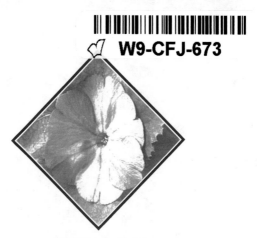

200 TIPS
for Growing
Beautiful
Perennials

Barbara Blossom Ashmun

CHICAGO
REVIEW
PRESS

**Library of Congress
Cataloging-in-Publication Data**

Ashmun, Barbara Blossom.
  200 tips for growing beautiful perennials /
by Barbara Blossom Ashmun.
      p.cm.
  Includes bibliographical references
      (p.) and index.
  ISBN 1-55652-278-9 (paper: alk. paper)
  1. Perennials. I. Title
SB434.A7851998
635.9'32—dc21   97-15712
                                            CIP

Published by Chicago Review Press,
Incorporated
814 North Franklin Street
Chicago, Illinois 60610
ISBN 1-55652-278-9
Printed in the United States of America
5 4 3 2 1

*In loving memory of my
stepmother, Celia Nemerow*

Contents

Acknowledgments

The idea for this book came one sweltering afternoon when it was too hot to garden and I was uncharacteristically lounging around in the lawn chairs with my thirteen-year-old neighbors, Gavin and Wes Younie. As usual, they were teasing me, poking fun at the long, windy title of the book I had just completed, *200 Tips for Growing Flowers in the Pacific Northwest.*

"Why don't you write a whole series, Barbara . . . *200 Tips for Growing Orchids, 200 Tips for Growing Geraniums* . . . ?" Gavin asked.

"Or asters, lilies, iris–how about grasses, or maybe spurges," I joked back. It seemed uproariously funny to consider writing a whole tips book about one genus.   Later, when I calmed down and cooled off, what seemed silly in the heat of the day actually made a lot of sense. A tips books on perennials or roses could be terrific–I'd been teaching very well attended classes on these topics for more than ten years.

So thanks, guys! Some of the best ideas come up when you're horsing around.

Over the years I've learned about perennials from hundreds of friends, teachers, students, clients, nursery owners, and growers. My deepest appreciation goes to the growers who've propagated these wonderful plants–the late Ed Wood, Grace Dinsdale, John and Susan Whittlesey, Al and Dot Rogers, Lorena M. Reid, Robyn Duback, Diana Reeck and Bill Janssen, Marietta and Ernie O'Byrne.

My thanks to Karim Winged Heart for salvaging those first clumps of hellebores from the bulldozers–they continue to bloom in my garden. To the late Connie Hansen, for showing me by example how one devoted woman could build a beautiful garden, even on very wet soil with horsetail. And to June Collins, who has generously grown perennials for me from seed exchanges in her productive greenhouse.

Heartfelt thanks to the many friends who've shared their gardens and love of perennials, heightening my appreciation for beauty, especially:

Donna and Tony Freeman, Virginia Plainfield, Sandy Childress, Ruth Mackey, Lori Delman, Ruth Kaufman,

Anita Morrison, Loie Benedict, Penny Vogel, Millie Kiggins, Jan Waltenmath, Stephen Carruthers, Gavin Younie, Margaret Willoughby, Dulcy Mahar, Fatima Vancura, Faith MacKaness, Betty and Tony Barker, and Elizabeth Marantz.

Introduction

My first perennials were presented to me on a shovel dripping dirt. My neighbor was dividing her Michaelmas daisies and wanted to share some.

"These are extra—I just can't stand to throw any away," she told me.

Then she gave me a tip for planting them.

"All you have to do is throw a little bonemeal at the bottom of the hole and they'll take off," she said.

I planted them that Saturday in 1974, and they bloomed that fall at the back of the border, blue and pink. Each year they returned and spread a little wider, and pretty soon I was dividing them and sharing them with other neighbors. In 1986, when I moved to two-thirds of an acre, divisions of those Michaelmas daisies traveled with me. I spread them out along a narrow rectangular bed to screen the lower wild field from the cultivated part of the backyard. They continue to bloom every fall—perennials are faithful.

Cottage pinks came to me just as unceremoniously. I was admiring some in a friend's garden, and she ripped a handful out of the ground. She held them out to me along with a planting tip.

"Just cut them back, enjoy the flowers in a vase, and stick the stems in some damp sand," she said. "Most of them will root down."

They did, and that was the beginning of my *Dianthus* collection.

I see a whole procession of friends and neighbors handing me slips of golden loosestrife and bearded iris rhizomes, starts of cranesbills and lily-of-the-valley. And along with the slips they handed me tips—cut it back hard in June, plant it in the shade, shelter it from wind. . . . Gardeners are a generous bunch, so there's a whole lot of sharing going on. A few admiring glances, and pretty soon out comes the shovel and you're going home with new plants and plenty of advice.

At first flowers dazzled me—brilliant red Oriental poppies and deep purple iris, yellow tickweeds and blue bellflowers. After a while I noticed the incredible leaves. Quilted hostas, lacy columbines, furry lamb's ears, and succulent sedums displayed their foliage in early spring, before the flowers opened. Many leaves were tinted, too–gray and blue-green, maroon and gold. Some were even spotted and marbled with silver and pink.

Fascinated, I began to read–books, magazines, catalogs–and joined plant societies to learn more. I raided the nurseries for perennials shown in English garden books and sent for plants by mail. Boxes arrived from North Carolina, Minnesota, California, crammed with mysterious roots, shoots, and bulbs.

I joined the Oregon State University Extension Service Master Gardener program and met an enormous tribe of impassioned gardeners and nursery owners.

Horticulture classes at several community colleges followed. Herb Orange, an innovative horticulture instructor at Clark College, noticed my fanatic interest in perennials and egged me on further.

"How would you like to create a perennial border on campus?" he asked. "If you design it, I'll find a budget for the plants and we'll ask a horticulture class to plant it. It'll be a great experience for all of us."

I leapt at the opportunity. We chose a site. I planned a border and started shopping for perennials. An entire class turned up the day of planting. I felt like a junior Gertrude Jekyll, pointing and shouting as students scurried to get plants situated.

Hundreds of borders later, I'm still fascinated by perennials. Old steadfast friends like peonies, daylilies, summer phlox, and coneflowers return year in and year out to mark the seasons and delight me with their color, texture, and fragrance. New cultivars arrive each year to entice me further–fancy-leaved coral bells and variegated lungworts, purple-leaved spurges and wine-colored hellebores. The pleasure of growing perennials and arranging them artfully is a lifelong passion that I hope you will share. I pass these tips along to you just as they were passed along to me, from gardener to gardener.

What Perennials Need to Thrive

Soil Preparation

1. **Invest your time to build a well-drained soil** *before* **planting, and you will earn long-term dividends–healthy, robust perennials.** I've lost more plants to death by drowning than anything else, due to my mucky clay soil that collects water and holds it fast. Some folks have sandy soil that drains too quickly and dries out. Amending soil with organic material– old manure, composted kitchen waste, composted sewage sludge, rotted leaves, sawdust, rabbit litter, spent straw, peat moss, and grass clippings–creates a balanced texture, spongy enough to

hold water, yet crumbly enough to let excess moisture run out and allow air and nutrients to reach the roots.

2 **At planting time amend your soil with aged chicken manure to improve soil texture and feed the perennials.** I dig a big hole and add a generous shovelful of well-rotted chicken manure, blending it into the existing soil. Since it's an organic fertilizer, manure improves imbalanced soils, breaking open clay-based soil and binding loose, sandy soil. In addition, chicken manure contains nitrogen, which nourishes the leaves of perennials, and phosphorus, which makes the flowers bigger and more profuse.

3 **Be careful to use well-rotted manure that has had a chance to age and cool down.** Fresh manure, and compost containing fresh manure, will burn the new roots of young perennials and can even damage emerging stems. To avoid that, your best bet is to use aged manure. In a pinch, place fresh manure at the bottom of a large planting hole, top it with at least eight inches of soil to serve as a barrier, and then plant your perennial. By the time the roots have grown down far enough, the manure will have ripened and cooled off.

Fertilizing

4 **Feed your perennials a modest amount of nitrogen to encourage the growth of foliage.** Blood meal, composted sewage sludge, cottonseed meal, bat guano, and poultry and rabbit manure are all rich in nitrogen. Some nitrogen is helpful to insure healthy green foliage, but don't overdo it or your perennials will grow lush leaves and stems at the expense of the flowers. Oversized plants are also more likely to keel over in heavy rain and wind.

5 **Be sure to add phosphorus to your soil to boost flower production.** Bonemeal and rock phosphate are both excellent sources of phosphorus. They break down slowly, thus nourishing perennials over a long period of time. I always add a handful of bonemeal to the hole at planting time, for a good start. In the spring I sprinkle bonemeal around the base of long-established perennials to renew them.

6 **When feeding perennials with a complete balanced fertilizer, select a formula with a high middle number for the most bloom-boosting**

phosphorus. Whether chemical or organic, boxes and sacks of fertilizer are labeled with three numbers that tell you the contents. For example, 5-10-5 means that the fertilizer is 5 percent nitrogen, 10 percent phosphorus, and 5 percent potassium (the rest is filler and spreader). Perennials benefit from all three ingredients, but a fertilizer highest in phosphorus will promote profuse flowering.

7 To save time, try slow-release granular fertilizers, especially when growing perennials in containers that are watered frequently. Slow-release fertilizers are easy to sprinkle in planting holes and ensure a steady supply of food during the growing season. For best results put the granules underground—left on the surface, they may oxidize on hot summer days and fail to benefit the perennials. Some formulas release over a period of three months and others over six months, so check the label for that information and choose the time frame that best suits the length of your growing season.

8 Experiment with liquid fertilizers to accelerate growth of new perennials. Liquid fertilizers applied directly to the leaves and root zones give plants a quick boost—you can almost watch the leaves grow. Available in both crystal and liquid forms, these fertilizers should be diluted with water in a sprinkling can according to the proportions specified in the directions. Stir well with a stick to make sure the fertilizer dissolves completely. Boxes of fertilizer that are paired with labor-saving hose-end sprayer bottles make this job easier and faster—I can fertilize my two-thirds acre garden this way in less than an hour.

Watering Methods

9 **The most efficient way to water perennials is with soaker hoses that weep.** To send the water where it will do the most good—down to the roots of perennials—lay down soaker hoses that slowly emit water. Commonly known as leaky hose, this type of soaker oozes moisture into the ground. Stay away from overhead watering systems. On hot days too much moisture is lost by evaporation. Also, the force of overhead sprinklers frequently knocks over tall perennials. While soakers seep only at the root zone, overhead sprinklers drench the foliage, and wet leaves are more susceptible to powdery mildew.

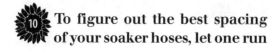 **10** **To figure out the best spacing of your soaker hoses, let one run**

for an hour and check the moisture pattern. For example, if the soil is damp a foot and a half to each side of a soaker, lay your hoses three feet apart; if it's damp only nine inches to each side, space your soakers a foot and a half apart. Several variables effect the moisture flow rate—the type of soaker, your soil composition, and water pressure.

11 Let the shape of your bed determine the way you arrange your soaker hoses. In a rectangular bed, it's simplest to lay soakers down in parallel straight lines, while in a circular or oval bed it's best to coil a soaker like a snail, starting at the center of the bed. To secure soakers around bends, make an oversized hairpin of flexible wire or an old wire hanger, and use it to pin the soaker down to the ground.

12 For the maximum conservation of water, cover your soakers with a few inches of fine-textured aged bark dust or finished compost. By mulching over the top of soakers, moisture will be held underground even more securely. When planting new perennials, be careful to move the mulch away from a buried soaker so as not to dig into the hose by accident.

13 **If you're impatient with how slowly soakers emit, punch extra holes on the underside with an ice pick.** Although gardening is said to teach us patience, this process may take years. Meanwhile, if you're frustrated, take an ice pick to your soakers to speed them up. If you want them to seep faster, punch the lower surfaces only. If you want them to soak and spray, perforate the soakers on all sides.

14 **You might also like ready-made soak-and-spray hoses, which water faster than leaky hose.** Soak-and-spray hoses are a lot like leaky hose, with the added feature of tiny holes at the top surface that send up a fine spray of water about 18 inches high. They're usually thinner, more flexible, and shorter-lived than leaky hose. Soak-and-spray hoses water faster and also help keep the lower foliage free of pests such as spider mites and aphids. However, water on the lower leaves may encourage powdery mildew.

15 **Attach timers to your watering spigots to regulate watering time.** Automatic watering devices are great time-savers for those of us with busy schedules. Deep watering encourages perennials to develop strong root systems and does more good than superficial sprinkling. For example, one hour weekly of steady watering is more beneficial than three 20-minute sessions spread out over seven days.

16 **Even though automatic watering systems save time, adjust them to reflect extremes in weather.** In times of drought or soaring heat, be sure to increase watering time to compensate for drying conditions. Similarly, if it rains a lot, turn off your watering system and let mother nature do the work. There's nothing sillier than a sprinkling system going full blast in the middle of a downpour.

17 **Make sure your perennials are getting enough water by being observant.** Even the best systems have problems from time to time, and it's important to troubleshoot, especially after a rough winter. If you have pop-up irrigation, make sure that all the heads are actively rising and spraying a full stream of water. Repair any that are stuck or plugged. Be aware that as perennials grow taller and wider during the growing season, they can easily block the path of a short pop-up sprinkler head. This is another reason to favor soakers.

Dig down gently with a trowel or your finger and assure yourself that the soil is damp a good six to eight inches deep, where the roots of perennials live. Scientific gardeners might enjoy using a water meter to determine soil moisture.

Mulch

18 **Mulch your perennial beds to conserve water and reduce weeds.** Proper spacing of young perennials is bound to leave gaps, and every bit of bare ground is an invitation to weeds. A mulch of compost, old manure, shredded leaves, or even grass clippings discourages weed seeds from germinating and holds moisture in the beds longer, making it that much easier to pull out the few stray weeds that sneak in. If you mulch with wood products such as bark dust or sawdust, add some nitrogen fertilizer to the ground, as these mulches consume nitrogen when they break down.

19 **Weed and water your beds before mulching.** A thorough clean-up and good soaking will get your perennials off to a good start before you lay down a layer of mulch. Otherwise existing weeds will continue to grow through the mulch, benefiting from its nutritional value and elbowing out your choice perennials.

20 **Weed early and save yourself from horticultural headaches.** Not only are young weeds easier to pull, but clearing them out early in the season will give perennials the breathing space they need to develop robustly. Weeds that begin flowering should signal you louder than a fire alarm. Remove them immediately, before they go to seed and become a cover crop.

21 **Allow perennials enough room to grow to maturity.** Check the ultimate size of a perennial before planting, and give it enough space to reach that size. When I had a city garden, I crowded too many perennials into a small space, and they grew meagerly. In my larger suburban garden where I spread the plants out more, they reward me by expanding to fill the more generous space.

Pest and Disease Prevention

22 **Plant perennials where there's good air circulation to prevent invasion of pests and diseases.** When I've grown hardy fuchsias in enclosed porches or tight courtyard corners where the air is stagnant, they usually succumb to whitefly. The same fuchsias growing in beds open to summer breezes stay healthy and vigorous. Summer phloxes flourish when they grow in island beds open to the air, while those cramped together against a fence have lower leaves full of powdery mildew. Lupines grown thickly in home gardens are soon covered with aphids and then coated with mildew, while those on windswept hillsides are the picture of health.

23 Clean up your garden to reduce damage from pests and diseases. Slugs and snails lurk in the leaf litter that naturally blows into the beds and borders each fall. Although the leaves protect the perennials from wind and cold through the winter, by spring they do greater damage by harboring pests. Rake them out as soon as the danger of severe cold has passed, and you'll have removed a natural breeding ground. Leaves with black spot should also be removed from the garden and destroyed.

24 Water early in the day to give the foliage a chance to dry off before evening falls. Damp leaves in cool temperatures are susceptible to powdery mildew, so it's best to avoid late afternoon and evening watering. Besides, doesn't it make sense to give the plants an early drink that they can use throughout the day?

25 Choose vigorous, healthy plants at the nursery. When shopping, select perennials with robust green leaves and vigorous, multiple stems. Avoid plants with signs of pests–notched leaves, indicating weevils, or pale foliage symptomatic of spider mites. Check the underside of the leaves for aphids, and stir the plant around a bit to see if whiteflies jump out. Don't worry too much about a slug in the pot–it probably means it's the juiciest plant in the flat–just leave the slug behind.

Laying Out Your Perennial Beds and Borders

Finding Your Point of View

26 **Plan some of your garden pictures by considering your windows as the frames.** Enjoy your garden while sitting at your desk or rinsing dishes at the kitchen sink by planning views from these places. Take time to stare out important windows and imagine the picture you'd like to see. Once you've created these compositions, make the most of enjoying them. For example, I have a great view of the backyard from my desk, but my computer table faced a blank wall—until I moved it beside the desk. Now I admire colorful perennial borders whether I'm typing or on the phone.

27 **Notice where you most enjoy sitting out in the garden, and plan your garden pictures from those points of view.** Without realizing it, many home owners create the best compositions near the front door, for the benefit of guests, neighbors, and passersby. Figure out where *you* are most likely to spend time outside–on the patio, on the front porch, in the shade of an apple tree–and then design a beautiful scene for yourself to soak up. Take your sketchbook outside, sit where you'd be looking from, and let your imagination soar.

28 **Use arches and arbors as opportunities to frame a view.** When peeking through a garden arch, always ask yourself, what enticing picture beckons me? An arch or arbor is a perfect opportunity to invite the viewer into a new scene. Think of the arch as a frame that encloses a small portion of the larger composition waiting on the other side, a sneak preview that whets your appetite for the show that unfolds when you step through.

29 **If you've already got a great composition in place, plunk**

down a bench at the best viewing position. For years my point of view was facedown to the dirt as I weeded or head-on into a tangled rosebush as I pruned. When I opened my garden to friends and clients, I bought chairs and benches so they could sit and enjoy the whole picture. Joining them to visit, I also began to appreciate the bigger view.

Don't be afraid that you'll neglect your weeding and pruning by sitting and staring. I believe the plants need this kind of admiration just as much as they need water and fertilizer.

Planning on Paper

30 **For more accuracy, draw up a scaled-down plan.** It's easy to misjudge distances and proportions. To get a clear idea of how much space you're working with, measure your garden and draw it to scale. Graph paper and an engineer's scale simplify this job, but even plain paper and a ruler will do. Draw the plan from a bird's point of view, and let one-fourth inch or one-half inch on paper represent one foot of garden space.

31 **Make numerous copies of your original plan, or overlay it with as many sheets of tracing paper as you need to experiment to your heart's content.** Give yourself lots of freedom to fool around with many versions of your design. Sometimes your first ideas will be your favorites, but often, as you explore, your later inventions will please you even more. Try out different shapes for your beds, borders, and paths until the whole picture comes together in a unified way.

Like doing warm-ups before you go for a run, doodling on paper stretches your mind. Sketch out the shapes of beds and borders roughly at first to see what pleases you most–curved or angular shapes, the soft flow of an ellipse or the crisp edge of a rectangle. Fiddle awhile before settling on a plan.

32 When planning perennial beds and borders, use tracing paper overlays to represent all four seasons. To design a four-season border, first draw up the shape of your bed to scale. Plan your fall border on the lowermost drawing. Then make a tracing paper overlay for each season. Place the first tracing paper overlay representing summer on top of your fall border, and sketch in perennials for summer. Next lay your spring border on top, and draw in those perennials that flower in spring. Finally, add the tracing paper overlay representing winter, superimpose it onto the first three layers, and sketch in your winter bloomers. Your composite will include all four seasons.

Shaping Spaces Out in the Garden

33 **Draw your design right on the ground for the most comprehensive picture.** I like to plan right out in the garden where I can best see the light patterns, the slope of the ground, and the relationship of the bed I'm designing to the rest of the garden. I use flexible hoses to shape curved beds and paths, stakes and string to mark straight edges. To draw circles, I use a stick-and-string compass. Sometimes I set stakes in the ground to represent key plants, but more often I arrange the plants aboveground in their containers and study them for awhile, visualizing how they will look in a year or two when they blend together. I might leave an arrangement out in the garden for several days, checking it from different angles and making adjustments as needed, until I'm satisfied and ready to plant.

Opening a Brand-New Bed

34 **To open new beds in the middle of turf, find the least toxic way to kill the grass.** Although many gardeners use herbicide to remove grass, the side effects on health and the environment are still uncertain and the cost of herbicide continues to mount. With a little lead time, it's safer and more economical to smother the grass by mechanical means. Lay down flattened cardboard or black plastic for a couple of months, and then remove them and prepare your bed for planting by turning the soil and amending with compost. Or lay newspaper down on top of the grass and begin composting on top of the newspaper with layers of leaves, kitchen waste, and manure. Wait a season or two for the compost to break down, then plant. For a quick fix, lay newspaper about an inch thick on top of the grass, add a couple of feet of well-aged compost, and plant immediately.

35 For instant raised island beds, build two-foot-tall stone walls for the frames and fill them with your favorite soil mix. Two ingenious gardeners I know salvaged large stones from a rocky country garden, doing their friends and themselves a favor. They hauled the stones home in their sturdy old pickup and stacked them, building two-foot-tall circular frames for a series of island beds. Then they filled the frames with a nutritious mix of manure and mushroom compost and planted perennials. What a transformation! In place of a monotonous front lawn, a colorful cottage garden now extends a warm welcome.

Elements of
Design

~~~~~~~

Color

36 **Think of perennials as dabs of color, and understand that it takes several plants to make a brush stroke.** To make an artistic garden, think of yourself as a painter and the perennials as paint. Use drifts of perennials to get a sweep of color. For example, if you want to accentuate a graceful S-curve that frames a border, repeat the same plant all along that edge to outline its shape in one color. To point to a distant vista, create a straight line of one color by planting a row of one kind of perennial all along the line. At Malleny, a Scottish estate garden, a long lavender hedge leads the way to a beautiful glasshouse.

37 **Let your compositions be a blending of prima donnas and supporting cast.** Showy flowers such as calla lilies, peonies, daylilies, iris, and lilies are the stars of flower borders. Let them shine, and surround them with a mist of subtler, smaller flowers. Try a stand of yellow daylilies with veil-like lavender meadow rue (*Thalictrum aquilegifolium*). Underpin bold red peonies with delicate blue cranesbills (*Geranium himalayense*) and plant lacy white *Geranium sanguineum* 'Album' at the feet of a blowsy pink peony. Let yellow pincushion flowers (*Scabiosa ochroleuca*) make a soft cloud around peach lilies let hazy lavender catmint (*Nepeta* 'Six Hills Giant') billow at the feet of a dark red rose. Plant hot orange Asiatic lilies in a cooling sea of blue flax (*Linum perenne*).

38 **Remember to use the full color palette: flowers, leaves, stems, and fruit.** *Penstemon* 'Husker Red' is a good example of a perennial that has it all. Newly emerging leaves and stems are deep burgundy, attracting immediate attention. In early summer, spikes of white flowers make an arresting contrast to the dark leaves. The blooms age and form intriguing maroon seedpods that decorate the stem like a long string of beads. 'Husker Red' offers color from spring to fall, thanks to its continuous transformation.

39 **Choose perennials with long bloom periods for lasting color.** Perennials like pasqueflower (*Pulsatilla vulgaris*) are showy but fleeting. Especially in small gardens, it's important to select plants that keep color for months. Lenten rose (*Helleborus orientalis*) steals the show as early as January in mild winters. Pink, cream, and even burgundy flowers continue into February, March, and April. 'Roy Davidson' lungwort (*Pulmonaria* 'Roy Davidson') also gets off to an early start, showing its first sky-blue flowers in February and lingering past Mother's Day.

40 **Pay close attention to your own unique reaction to color. Let your eyes and your heart be your guides.** The garden is one place where we can please ourselves first, and color is a personal choice. For one gardener, red is as exciting as a gift of roses; for another, it's as irritating as a red flag to a bull. White soothes some and bores others. Magenta makes me want to shout with delight, but you might scream with horror.

Get acquainted with *your* emotional responses to colors. A vibrant composition of mustard yellow, hot pink, and brilliant orange may thrill or alarm you. Respect your feelings and create the color compositions that make you happy. Be open to the likelihood that your taste will change over time. Simply stay aware, and have fun playing with the infinite possibilities of color.

41 **To better understand the effects of color, treat yourself to a huge box of crayons.** Studying color is a lifetime occupation, and the color wheel showing the six hues—red, orange, yellow, green, blue, and purple—is only a beginner's sampler. Three primary colors, red, yellow, and blue, are the building blocks. To arrive at the secondary colors, mix red and yellow for orange, blue and yellow for green, and red and blue for purple. Looking at the wheel you will see that the three primary colors form a triangle—so do the three secondary colors. Each secondary color sits between its primary parents.

What is not evident from the six basic colors becomes clearer when you arrange the crayons in a 64-count crayon box in the same order as the color wheel. Each color has darker shades and lighter tints. For example, the green crayon has darker kin—pine green and forest green—and lighter relatives—sea green and spring green. Yellow-green, olive green, and yellow-green are intermediate colors that lie between green and its brighter neighbor, yellow. As blue approaches green, green-blue, aquamarine, blue-green, and turquoise arise. In the garden, there's even more variation. Notice these intriguing subtleties and your understanding of color will deepen.

42 **For the subtlest color scheme, work with shades and tints of just one color.** If you have the discipline and restraint to try a monochromatic color scheme, you'll learn all about the range of that particular color. Pink, a tint of red, can lean toward lavender, peach, or blush depending on how much blue, yellow, or white it contains. It can be as pale as lip gloss or as deep as rosé wine.

Bloom shape becomes more apparent when the color scheme is simplified. Spikes and trumpets, globes and plumes stand out more without the distraction of many hues vying for our attention. Leaf texture also gains importance when color is limited. The best-known monochromatic garden is at Sissinghurst Castle, where flowers in all shades of white are supported by green and gray foliage, creating a mood of serenity.

43 **Pay attention to the way light influences color in the garden.** When it comes to flowers, the opacity or transparency of the petals affects color. A double red rose with velvety petals will appear much darker than a red poppy that lets light pour through its papery petals. The luminous quality of tree peonies and single forms of roses, herbaceous peonies, and anemones has a lot to do with the way light and color work together.

Color changes too depending on whether plants are placed in sun or shade. Pale pink seems to glow in the shade. Strong sun bleaches pink to a paler tint. Similarly, on an overcast day color appears more radiant than on a bright day.

44 **For the most electricity, pair opposite colors on the color wheel: purple and yellow, blue and orange, red and green.** Extreme opposites provide the greatest contrast. Plant purple spires of great bellflower (*Campanula latifolia*) beside yellow Jerusalem sage (*Phlomis fruticosa*). Pair deep purple 'Caesar's Brother' Siberian iris with bright yellow spurge (*Euphorbia palustris*) for a striking spring vignette.

A carpet of blue forget-me-not beneath orange poppies, blue false indigo (*Baptisia australis*) with orange spurge (*Euphorbia griffithii* 'Fireglow'), or blue lily-of-the-Nile (*Agapanthus* hybrids) beside *Crocosmia* 'Lucifer' make a striking picture.

Red and green combinations require only red flowers in a nest of green foliage. Mass red oriental poppies along a low stone wall; their crepe-papery flowers and bold, hirsute foliage are showy enough. Red astilbe underplanted by evergreen deer fern make a simple yet strong combination.

45 **White flowers are among the brightest—use them where you intentionally want a magnetic picture or to liven up a bland composition.** Don't be misled into thinking that white is a neutral color. Because it reflects so much light, it calls a lot of attention to itself, like a glowing beacon. Especially when contrasted with dark colors, including the green of foliage, white stands out like stars in the night sky.

But let's say that you've gone overboard on pink—you've planted pink roses, pink lilies, and pink *Heucherella* 'Bridget Bloom'. You might add touches of double white feverfew, white *Geranium sanguineum* 'Album', and white *Veronica* 'Icicle' to make the picture sparkle.

If, on the other hand, you have some clashing colors that need mediation, don't introduce white—it will only fan the flames, jumping out to attract yet more attention. You'd do better to add blue or cream flowers to calm things down. Gray, blue-green, and variegated foliage (which translates as cream) also serve as effective buffers.

46 **For a vibrant, crisp composition, be bold with white and red.** Each brilliant red flower of 'Firebird' beardtongue (*Penstemon* 'Firebird') has a white throat that begs to be echoed by white roses, white balloon flowers (*Platycodon grandiflorus* 'Albus'), or white summer phlox (*Phlox paniculata* 'World Peace').

'St. Mary's' sun rose (*Helianthemum* 'St. Mary's) is a favorite for its clean white flowers that sparkle against dark green leaves in early summer. What a lovely accent it makes beneath red 'Othello' roses! Similarly, Jupiter's beard (*Centranthus ruber* 'Alba') weaves its fluffy white columns between the red shrub roses in a mixed border like lace trim on a velvet gown.

47 **For a warm, rousing picture, be brazen with red, yellow, and orange.** It takes pluck to work with fiery colors, but with a little experience, you develop a taste for heat. The key is to balance strength with strength—intense yellow with equally strong red and vibrant-enough orange. A strong red will drown out a pale yellow; too weak an orange will be lost beside a saturated yellow.

Red-orange *Crocosmia* 'Lucifer' meets its match with mustard yellow 'Coronation Gold' yarrow (*Achillea* 'Coronation Gold') but will overwhelm creamy *Achil-*

lea 'Hoffnung'. Similarly, deep orange daylilies strike a good balance with bright yellow *Ligularia* 'The Rocket', but apricot daylilies require the gentler yellow of dusty meadow rue (*Thalictrum speciosissimum*).

48 **To knit strong colors together, add touches of intermediate tones.** Move from intense shades of a color to its paler tints in very small increments, so that the picture blends together like an artful watercolor. Brilliant orange and red montbretias and hot yellow yarrows can be melded together by flowers that are slightly less intense– buttery yellow Anthemis 'Wargrave' and yellow *Nepeta govaniana*, with delicate flowers. Add some lighter orange chrysanthemums and coral 'Glow' pokers to help smooth the colors together.

49 **For a rich composition, expand each color by adding flowers in shades and tints of the original hue.** Instead of picking out a tune with single notes, let out all the stops and play complex chords. For example, if blue and yellow are your mainstays for early summer, start with a medium blue peach-leaved bellflower (*Campanula persicifolia*) and add lighter-tinted milky bellflower (*Campanula lactiflora*) and 'Blue Giant' speedwell (*Veronica* 'Blue

Giant'). Darken down to 'Midnight' speedwell (*Veronica* 'Midnight') and dark blue forms of Siberian, Japanese, or bearded iris.

Do the same with yellow. Choose a medium yellow Siberian iris, like 'Butter and Sugar', and darken down with globeflower (*Trollius europaeus*) or cushion spurge (*Euphorbia epithymoides*). Lighten up with buttery Jerusalem sage (*Phlomis russeliana*) and creamy Argentine blue-eyed grass (*Sisyrinchium striatum*).

50 Blue and pink are sure to please, and will come to life with touches of purple and white. Pink hollyhock mallow (*Malva alcea* 'Fastigiata') and blue Carpathian bellflower (*Campanula carpatica*), pink evening primrose (*Oenothera speciosa*) and blue balloon flower (*Platycodon grandiflorum*) are harmonious companions for summer. Add purple 'Midnight Blue' beardtongue (*Penstemon* 'Midnight Blue') and white Santa Barbara daisy (*Erigeron karvinskianus*) to enliven the picture.

51 Feeling daring? Plant punchy magenta with equally jazzy companions. Brilliant flowers can handle strong partners. Paired with pale yellow, magenta looks garish and domineering, but place it beside bright yellow or yellow-green and it sparkles, having met its match. Let moss campion (*Lychnis coronaria*) glow near lady's mantle (*Alchemilla mollis*); plant *Geranium subcaulescens* with a bright yellow buttercup, *Ranunculus gramineus,* and rejoice in their combined radiance.

Pair *Geranium psilostemon* with annual *Nicotiana langsdorfii* for an arresting composition. This cranesbill alone is guaranteed to stop traffic, its round magenta flowers centered by a black eye. Contrasting spikes of *Nicotiana langsdorfii*, graced by delicate chartreuse bells, make everyone linger for a second look.

When you notice that magenta is a close neighbor of purple, which loves bright yellow, this combination of magenta and yellow will be less surprising.

52 Marry brilliant colors to more reserved partners for subtler compositions. Magenta *Geranium psilostemon* may be paired with blue-violet catmint (*Nepeta sibirica*) or Russian sage (*Perovskia atriplicifolia*) and a deep crimson-purple rose such as *Rosa rugosa* 'Roseraie de L'Hay' or *Rosa rugosa* 'Hansa'. The more muted lavender and deeper crimson allow the cranesbill to shine but not shout. A backdrop of variegated ornamental grasses such as *Miscanthus sinensis*

'Variegatus' will also have a quieting effect.

Similarly, moss campion (*Lychnis coronaria*) will glow softly in the company of blue-violet and pink perennials–balloon flowers (*Platycodon grandiflorum*) and hollyhock mallow (*Malva alcea* 'Fastigiata'), for example. And 'Bowles Mauve' wallflower (*Erysimum* 'Bowles Mauve') cools down the magenta flowers of bloody cranesbill (*Geranium sanguineum*). Whatever you do, avoid magenta and pure white–the results will be blinding.

53 Experiment with color to discover all the possibilities–be willing to break the rules. I once held a belief that blue and green clashed until I saw a friend wearing a turquoise shirt with chartreuse pants. The combination was dazzling. When I stopped to analyze the colors, I was really looking at blue-green contrasting with yellow-green, and it worked beautifully–it was a version of blue and yellow, which is always successful, jazzed up by the addition of green to both colors. You could translate this discovery from clothing to garden design by combining blue-green and yellow-green hosta foliage or by pairing blue-green hosta foliage with yellow-green flowers–say *Hosta* 'Krossa Regal' with lady's mantle (*Alchemilla mollis*).

I thought that pink and orange would do battle until I saw peach, pink, and creamy yellow Asiatic lilies cavorting between pink roses. Pink and light orange Peruvian lilies (*Alstroemeria ligtu*) also surprised me pleasantly, in the company of yellow lemon lily (*Hemerocallis lilioasphodelus*). So did pink and orange zinnias and dahlias, blending together like a showy sunset.

54 **Juxtapose pots of perennials at the nursery, arrange flower bouquets, and study paintings and fabrics, all with an eye for new possibilities.** An easy way to try colors out is at the nursery–stare before you spend. Gather up potential mates and study them in a group for a while to see if their arrangement pleases you. In your garden, cut flowers for bouquets, and simply move compatible companions closer to each other.

Beautiful linens, clothing, even wallpaper will give you new ideas about color combinations. The more you observe, the better you'll understand color, just like spending time with a favorite friend and getting better acquainted.

55 **Plant perennials with blue-green foliage to cool down orange and hot pink flowers and mediate between clashing colors.** In a sunny border, blue-green rue (*Ruta graveolens*) makes a gorgeous patina accent, topped with small yellow flowers in summer. Try a hedge of rue in front of a medley of roses to unite them.

Blue oat grass (*Helictotrichon sempervirens*), with narrow, subtle foliage, makes a soothing splash of cool color toward the front of a border. In shade, choose from many blue-green hostas for the same effect–my favorites are Siebold's hosta, classically beautiful, and the amazingly husky 'Krossa Regal'.

56 Use purple and burgundy-leaved perennials to make exotic dark accents in borders that beg for excitement. The rich dark leaves of purple sage, purple-leaved loosestrife (*Lysimachia ciliata* 'Purpurea'), and 'Starfire' summer phlox (*Phlox paniculata* 'Starfire') create a stir in the garden well before their flowers appear. In spring I count on the maroon leaves of *Penstemon* 'Husker Red' and *Sedum* 'Mohrchen' to echo the vibrant wine leaves of a 'Royal Purple' smoke tree nearby.

57 In shade, keep the dark-leaved beauties from disappearing by giving them a brighter foil for contrast. *Heuchera* 'Palace Purple' and

'Brunette' bugbane (*Cimicifuga* 'Brunette') are great for spicing up shady borders. However, 'Palace Purple' is such a dark shade of bittersweet chocolate that it can blend into the soil color. An underplanting of green London pride (*Saxifraga umbrosa*) makes 'Palace Purple' more visible.

Let 'Brunette' bugbane show off its gorgeous dissected dark leaves by planting it in a sea of brighter green. A ground cover of low-growing bishop's hat (*Epimedium species* and hybrids) or 'Biokovo' cranesbills would accomplish the necessary color contrast.

58 Try planting dusky *Ligularia* 'Desdemona' to dress up a drab shady bed. Showing off new foliage and stems the color of beets, *Ligularia dentata* 'Desdemona' expands until its leaves are saucer sized. Mature foliage turns green but retains a purple underside. Three feet tall by midsummer, 'Desdemona' is topped by unlikely orange daisies. Protect it from slugs that gobble the new leaves, and provide lots of water and deep shade.

59 The mysterious leaves of black mondo grass (*Ophiopogon planiscapus* 'Nigrescens') show up best emerging from a carpet of gray. In Jan Waltenmath's Portland garden, black mondo grass is surrounded by gray pussytoes (*Antennaria dioica*)–the contrast of foliage colors benefits both plants. The pussytoes grow in a subtle, flat mat, punctuated by the moppetlike tufts of black mondo grass. Woolly thyme or *Sedum spathulifolium* would provide similar contrast.

60 Pair white-variegated foliage with white flowers to create sophisticated color echoes. These are especially welcome in shade. Leaves patterned with white beg for an accompaniment of white blossoms–the flowers and foliage resonate, enhancing each other's beauty. To illuminate the dark floor of woodland gardens, try variegated Solomon's seal (*Polygonatum odoratum* 'Variegatum') with white columbines, primroses, and astilbes. Similarly, plant *Hosta* 'Francee', its leaves crisply outlined in white, with a froth of white sweet woodruff and lily-of-the-valley.

61 To warm up and brighten cool, shady borders, pair yellow-variegated foliage with yellow flowers. *Hosta* 'Frances Williams' has generous green leaves outlined in yellow. You can emphasize these margins by planting yellow daylilies and European globeflowers (*Trollius europaeus*) nearby.

Hakonechloa macra 'Aureola' is a popular shade-loving grass with golden leaves striped green, low enough to edge the front of a border, spilling bright color onto a path all spring, summer, and fall. Use it to lead the way up a shady bank or draw you further along a darkened woodland path. Echo its golden leaves with the small yellow flowers of bishop's hat (*Epimedium* x *versicolor*).

62 Pair yellow-variegated foliage with yellow flowers for cheering compositions in full sun. *Sedum alboroseum* 'Medio-Variegatum' makes a brilliant accent, its succulent creamy yellow leaves outlined in green. Plant yellow marguerites (*Anthemis tinctoria* 'Wargrave') or pokers (*Kniphofia* 'Little Maid' or 'Primrose Beauty') to echo the sedum's foliage color. The substantial sedum anchors the more ethereal flowers.

Iris pseudacorus 'Variegata' and *Iris pallida* 'Aurea Variegata' are distinguished by blades of green foliage striped with buttery yellow. Either is lovely accompanied by a froth of lady's mantle (*Alchemilla mollis*).

63 Combine burgundy-variegated foliage with pink, peach, or wine flowers for a rich union. The new, expanding clan of coral bells offers a host of gorgeous leaves reminiscent of Rex begonias. Tinted with burgundy, silver, pink, and chocolate, they have names as enticing as jewels–'Ruby Veil', 'Amethyst Mist', and 'Stormy Seas'.

These unusual perennials make striking partners for a variety of flowers. Study their iridescent patterns and find flowers that echo their tints. In shade, try them with pink masterwort (*Astrantia major* 'Rosea') or darker burgundy masterwort (*Astrantia carniolica* 'Rubra'). Add astilbes in pink, peach, and even dark red tones. In morning sun (strong afternoon sun may burn the leaves of fancy-foliaged coral bells), smaller-flowered daylilies in related hues are good choices–plum-toned 'Little Missie', 'Little Lassie', and 'Little Grapette'.

64 **Don't get too carried away with variegated perennials or you will end up with a crazy quilt.** It's tempting to plant every kind of intriguingly marked plant, but your eye will soon tire of so much commotion. Think of variegated leaves as accessories, and use them as sparingly as you would jewelry. One gem, shade-loving *Tovara virginiana*, has elliptical green leaves marked with striking red chevrons. Let this foliage star by planting lacy ferns nearby. To emphasize the red chevrons, echo their color with red-flowering astilbe. The dissected leaves of astilbe will contrast with the *Tovara* without distracting.

Texture

65 **Select foliage and flowers with varying textures to make your borders more interesting.** The woolly leaves of mulleins (*Verbascum species*) and lamb's ears (*Stachys lanata*) are a pleasure to regard and to touch. Quilted hosta leaves, feathery fennel foliage, jagged cardoon, leathery bergenia, and succulent sedums make striking textural accents.

Flowers too add details that take us beyond color–crepe-papery poppies, prickly globe thistles, velvety auricula primroses, and silky blue flax add textural touches to the garden.

Form

66 **Give foliage form its due–leaves are important a lot longer than flowers, contributing a wonderful range of shapes to beds and borders.** Consider the elliptical foliage of hosta, lady's mantle's (*Alchemilla mollis*) lobed leaves, the linear blades of iris, and the heart-shaped leaves of bishop's hat (*Epimedium pinnatum*). Notice how pleasing these bold forms are in contrast to the delicate flowers, how they anchor the beds. Shapely leaves ground the more diaphanous swirls of color and give the eye a resting place between floral orgies.

67 Plant evergreen perennials that bloom early for a double shot of winter cheer. Winter is when we most need the garden's green hope. Leaves carpeting the cold ground remind us that flowers will soon arrive. *Bergenia cordifolia* blooms in early spring, or even late winter in mild climates. Large leathery leaves make it prominent at the front of a border, and new hybrids with white, rosy pink, lilac, and red flowers add variety to the original magenta. Donkeytail spurge (*Euphorbia myrsinites*), a gray-leaved draper, shows its bright yellow flowers in February.

Four species of hellebore sport evergreen leaves and winter blooms: Corsican hellebore (*Helleborus corsicus*), with serrated dark green leaves and greenish yellow flowers; Lenten rose (*Helleborus orientalis*), with palmate leaves and pink, maroon, and cream-colored flowers; Christmas rose (*Helleborus niger*), with dark leaves and white flowers; and bearsfoot hellebore (*Helleborus foetidus*), with pinwheel-shaped leaves and greenish yellow flowers edged with red.

68 **Plant plenty of evergreen perennials that bloom in spring—they make great edgers.** Evergreen candytuft (*Iberis sempervirens*) with white flowers and bishop's hat (*Epimedium* species and hybrids) with heart-shaped leaves and flowers in pink, yellow, white, and even lavender are spring bloomers. Mrs. Robb's spurge (*Euphorbia robbiae*) boasts glossy green rosettes and bright yellow flowers that open in March. Dozens of coral bell cultivars offer evergreen leaves and dainty spikes of red, pink, and white flowers.

Tough as nails, magenta *Geranium macrorrhizum* is not only evergreen but drought resistant and shade tolerant. Shade-loving London pride (*Saxifraga umbrosa*) is also great. Plant it at the edge of a border or as a moderately spreading ground cover between larger plants. Its rosettes of dark green leaves are topped by spikes of blush-pink flowers in spring.

69 **Save room for evergreen perennials that bloom in summer.** Cottage pinks (*Dianthus plumarius*), beloved for their fragrance, also keep their silvery leaves year-round. Flowers are double, single, and even fringed, in shades of white, pink, red, and wine.

Gray lamb's ears (*Stachys lanata*) and blue-green rue (*Ruta graveolens*) hold their leaves in all but the harshest winters. Lamb's ears' small magenta flowers nestle in its woolly stems, while rue's bright yellow flowers sit at the top of the decorative foliage.

70 **Plant evergreen perennials with unusually colored foliage to enliven border edges.** Low-growing cream-variegated Japanese sedge (*Carex morrowii* 'Variegata') makes a bright accent along a path year-round. Even more brilliant, golden 'Ogon' sweet flag looks very much like an ornamental grass, only its leaf blades are wider. 'Ogon' is also very tolerant of wet feet. And blue oat grass (*Helictotrichon sempervirens*) keeps its blue-gray leaves year-round, as does deep green 'Arp' rosemary.

71 **Plant low-growing evergreen ferns at the front of shade borders for permanent foliage interest.** Hart's tongue fern (*Asplenium scolopendrium*) has unusual strap-shaped leaves that are shiny green, nice and bright in shady borders. It's a good size (one to two feet tall) for the front or middle of a border.

Deer fern (*Blechnum spicant*) is also low, with handsome deep green leaves arranged in satisfying symmetry. The little hard fern (*Blechnum penna-marina*) is a dainty treasure, only six inches tall—perfect for carpeting the edges of shade beds or covering ground beneath shrubs. In New Zealand I saw it grown as a sweet ground cover on infrequently traveled shady paths—I imagined elves treading lightly on its finely textured leaves.

72 **Plant medium-sized evergreen ferns towards the center of shade borders for year-round greenery.** The interesting evolution of autumn fern (*Dryopteris erythrosora*) makes it one of my favorite woodland plants. The young unfurling fronds are a surprising coppery pink. Later in summer the foliage turns dark green. In fall the leaves are tinted bronze. Even though it's tall enough for midborder, I plant the autumn fern at the front edge to best appreciate its color changes.

The crested soft shield fern (*Polystichum setiferum* 'Rotundatum cristatum') is popular for its lacy texture and fresh green color. It's a beautiful foil for masterworts (*Astrantia major*), hostas, and astilbes.

73 **Pay attention to the variety of flower shapes, and use them to create interesting patterns.** Spikes of penstemon, lavender, monkshood, foxtail lily (*Eremurus*), poker (*Kniphofia*), mallow, hollyhock, delphinium, and speedwell (*Veronica*) contribute vertical thrust to beds and borders. Trumpet-shaped lilies, daylilies, and daffodils add substantial blocks of color and elegant profiles. Globe-shaped flowering onion (*Allium*), lily-of-the-Nile (*Agapanthus*), peonies, and poppies offer roundness, while yarrow and Japanese iris, which flower on the horizontal plane, form flat plates.

Contrast

74 For dramatic effects, juxtapose different flower shapes. Picture lily trumpets contrasting with flowering onion lollipops or delphiniums rocketing beside saucers of horizontal yarrow to visualize the exciting tension of opposites. Spikes of speedwell and round peonies, spires of purple toadflax (*Linaria purpurea*) and circular poppies, linear lavender and globose pink evening primroses (*Oenothera speciosa*) accomplish the same end.

Repetition

75 To maximize harmony, repeat similar flower shapes. Looking at a host of same-shaped flowers in related colors brings the subtle differences to light. The sameness creates unity, the differences diversity, thus pleasing and intriguing the eye. In a sunny border, blend spikes of foxtail lily and pokers in shades of orange, peach, and yellow. The foxtail lily's taller, wider, and more feathery flowers contrast in texture with the pokers' denser ones. At the same time, their colors and forms echo one another.

In shade, mix plumes of astilbe and goatsbeard, which have similar flowers and foliage, varying mainly in size–the goatsbeard is the larger cousin. Add some bugbane (*Cimicifuga* species), with similarly dissected leaves. Its bottlebrush-shaped flowers offer contrast.

Creating Perennial Borders

~ ✂✂ ~

One-Season Borders

76 For the strongest color impact, design a one-season border. One of the most exciting borders I've ever seen was a symphony of fall color. Blue-violet lacecap hydrangea (*Hydrangea serrata villosa*), 'Bluebird' rose of Sharon (*Hibiscus syriacus* 'Bluebird'), blue fall-flowering sage (*Salvia patens, Salvia uliginosa, Salvia pitcherii*), pink and white anemone (*Anemone japonica*), deep blue willow gentian (*Gentiana asclepiadea*), lavender Joe-Pye weed (*Eupatorium purpureum*), burgundy, pink, and purple beard-tongue (*Penstemon* 'Garnet', *Penstemon beckia nitida*) sparkled in the autumn sun. Because no gaps were left from earlier-blooming perennials, the color impact was intense.

77 Divide your garden into separate spaces, and try different color schemes within them. Garden rooms allow you more freedom to experiment with color. A sunny space could be devoted to warm colors–orange, red, and yellow–with no fear of pink or mauve intruding to clash. A shady space might be planted with pastel pink, light blue, and creamy white perennials, with an occasional purple accent. Magenta and chartreuse flowers with plum-colored foliage might be perfect to enliven a gray slate patio. A blue garden with touches of white could make a small entry courtyard appear more spacious.

78 Experiment freely with color schemes that change with the seasons. Since perennials bloom for a limited time, it's possible to have many color schemes within the same border. Blue, pink, and yellow seem perfect for spring fever. Try blending blue lungwort (*Pulmonaria* species), Jacob's ladder (*Polemonium* species), and blue columbine with pink thrift (*Armeria maritima*), pink hyacinths, and 'Nora Barlow' columbine. Plant yellow daffodils, yellow columbine, and leopard's bane (*Doronicum caucasum*) to complete the picture.

Heat up the summer color by adding daylilies, pokers, montbretias, tickweed, and blanketflowers in shades of warmer yellow and red. For fall, return to the cool colors by combining blue, purple, burgundy, and pink Michaelmas daisies with white boltonia, pink obedience plant, pink 'Carmen' sedum, and dwarf asters in similar hues.

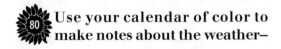

79 Keep a calendar of color to learn when and how long perennials bloom. Keep a small spiral notebook handy, and list perennials as they bloom, month by month, also noting their continuity from month to month. You'll see that *Gaura lindheimerii* flowers nonstop from July through October. Its long flower spikes expand ceaselessly, offering hundreds of white flowers flushed with pink, like many tiny butterflies. By contrast, *Gillenia trifoliata*, with equally delicate white flowers, comes and goes within one month in early summer. In a large garden, you may choose to grow both, but in a smaller one where you must make the most of every plant, the choice is evident.

80 Use your calendar of color to make notes about the weather—

you'll learn how changing weather patterns affect bloom periods. Over the years you'll notice changes in onset of bloom time as well as length of bloom period. An especially warm winter will bring perennials into flower earlier than usual, while a cool, wet spring may delay bloom time. The same perennial that flowers for eight weeks in a cool, damp summer may flower itself to a frazzle in a few weeks of blistering heat.

Even if you don't keep a calendar of color, a few scribbles on your desk calendar will be instructive. A friend notes the weather by sketching rain clouds or a shining sun on each day's page, and occasionally she jots down the high and low temperatures of the day. At the end of each year, she scans the annual pattern and compares it with past years' trends to see the bigger picture.

81 **Use a finding list to become familiar with the specific nature of each perennial you wish to grow.** Take a sheet of paper and make several columns headed as follows: Botanical Name, Common Name, Color, Bloom Time, Height and Spread, Foliage, Remarks.

As you learn about perennials that you'd like to include in your border, note their characteristics under the appropriate column. Under "Foliage" describe the leaf color, if it's gray, wine, or variegated; or the leaf texture, if it's woolly, silky, or succulent.

The "Remarks" column is an all-purpose place to keep track of the perennial's needs—for shade or sun, for moisture, for staking or slug bait. Note here companions that bloom at the same time or compatible plants that like the same growing conditions.

Use a finding list to gather up perennials for any particular situation. Let's say you're designing a blue and yellow border. Simply highlight blue and yellow flowers under your "Color" column, and consider their bloom season, height, and spread to determine how to arrange them.

82 Make cutouts of perennials from colored construction paper to help you visualize the balance of color within a border. Create small movable icons to represent the perennials you plan to incorporate in your border, and label them by name. Add any other information you need on the cutout—height, bloom period, shape of flower (abbreviate the words if your cutouts are small). Then shuffle them around and experiment with various combinations, keeping in mind contrast of color and flower shape and simultaneous bloom periods. Repeat colors and shapes within the larger border to unify the design. When you're satisfied with the results, glue your cutouts in place for the finished plan.

All-Season Borders

To design an all-season border, choose clusters of perennials from each season, aiming for a series of seasonal vignettes. In an effort to balance all four seasons democratically, it's easy to scatter the color around, helter-skelter. Don't do this. With a little more effort you can design a series of small seasonal compositions within the larger all-season border. For example, plan several groups of pink peonies, purple Siberian iris, and blue-violet cranesbills (*Geranium himalayense*) for early summer; a few drifts of pink summer phlox (*Phlox paniculata*), blue-violet Frikart's aster (*Aster x frikartii*), and white coneflower (*Echinacea purpurea* 'White Swan') for midsummer; and masses of brown-eyed Susan (*Rudbeckia triloba*), purple beardtongue (*Penstemon* 'Blackbird'), and purple monkshood (*Aconitum carmichaelii*) for autumn.

As groups of summer-flowering perennials come into bloom, nearby fall bloomers form buds, preparing for the next wave of color. As perennials bloom and wane, floral color flashes through the border like fireworks, while foliage remains as constant as the night sky.

Mixed Borders

84 **When you're ready for the ultimate challenge, plan a mixed border.** Melding trees, shrubs, perennials, vines, annuals, and bulbs requires some finesse. For starters, become knowledgeable about the ultimate sizes and cultural requirements of plants that you're considering. A sizable tree will eventually turn your sunny border into a shady one. This is fine if you want to grow shade lovers, but you may also lose a lot of moisture to the tree roots and be limited to perennials that can take dry shade. To minimize drought, stay away from surface-rooting trees in favor of deep-rooting species. And if you don't want shade, forego trees and stick with loosely branching shrubs.

85 **Keep an eye on proportions between trees, shrubs, and herbaceous plants in the mixed border.** Balance is important in a mixed border. Select only a few trees, a modest number of shrubs, and generous numbers of perennials, bulbs, and annuals, just as you would have fewer sofas than chairs in your living room, and fewer tables than framed pictures. Expect to prune your trees and shrubs to keep them within bounds. Fertilize, mulch, and water the perennials, bulbs, and annuals so they don't get starved by the bigger plants. Expect to move some of the smaller plants as the bigger ones spread out to occupy more space.

Back, Middle, and Front of the Border

86 Divide your border into three sections for easier planning: the front, the middle, and the back. In general, short plants belong at the front of the border, medium-height plants in the middle, and tall plants at the back. Penciling in broken lines to define these three areas will remind you to plan the heights appropriately.

To avoid a staircase look, break the rule of short, medium, and tall by interspersing a few taller plants toward the front and middle of the border, choosing transparent plants that don't eclipse their shorter companions. Fisherman's wand (*Dierama pulcherrimum*), *Gaura lindheimerii*, meadow rue (*Thalictrum aquilegifolium*), and queen-of-the-prairie (*Filipendula rubra*) are tall, veil-like plants that serve this purpose.

87 Always allow at least three feet of empty space behind a border. Perennial borders require ongoing grooming, weeding, fertilizing, and mulching. Give yourself room to tend the plants at the back of the border with ease by leaving a path at the rear. This is even more critical if your border is backed by a hedge that needs clipping, shrubs that need pruning, or a fence that needs maintenance.

Edges

88 **The front of the border makes the first impression—plant it with perennials that have good manners.** Tidy, compact plants at the edge will make your borders crisp and orderly. In sunny places, try compact forms of lavender ('Hidcote', 'Munstead'), bergenia, thrift (*Armeria maritima*), compact cranesbills (*Geranium renardii, Geranium sanguineum* 'Striatum', *Geranium cantabrigiense*). In shade, masterwort (*Astrantia major*), Lenten rose (*Helleborus orientalis*), small and medium-size hostas ('Abiqua Blue Edger', 'Gold Edger', 'Halcyon', 'Honeybells'), and coral bells (*Heuchera sanguinea*) make good anchors for the front of borders.

89 **To create a strong separation between a border and lawn, plant low evergreen hedges.** Traditional bor-

ders edged with clipped dwarf boxwood
are often found in estate gardens. The
strong lines that result give a crisp edge,
suggesting formality. These minihedges
also give support to front-of-the-border
perennials that might otherwise sprawl
into the grass. Evergreen germander or
compact forms of santolina or hyssop
may be clipped to construct even shorter
frames for the front of the border.

Fillers for Gaps

90 **While your perennials are growing up, plant the gaps with annuals and biennials.** Perennials take a
few years to fill out, and meanwhile you
don't have to stare at bare dirt and suffer. Relaxed annuals such as cosmos,
flowering tobacco (*Nicotiana* hybrids),
spider flower (*Cleome*), red flax (*Linum
rubrum*), 'Victoria Blue' salvia, larkspur,
and love-in-a-mist (*Nigella*) are compatible with perennials in style and form.
Stay away from blocky and garish annuals such as African marigolds, red
salvia, and zonal geraniums–they'll
shout for attention and distract from the
border's unity.

91 **Plant suitable companions to
cover spaces left by spring-
blooming perennials that go dormant.**

Sun-loving oriental poppies make their splash in spring but disappear by mid-summer. Interplant daylilies, obedient plant (*Physostegia virginiana*), or baby's breath to camouflage the bare spots. Shade-loving glacier lilies (*Erythronium*) and bleeding heart (*Dicentra spectabile*) die down after flowering. Plant willow gentians, astilbes, ferns, or hostas between the earlier bloomers to cover the gaps.

Island
Beds

⋙⋘

92 **Plant island beds with taller plants toward the center.** Is land beds are freestanding and viewed from all sides, in contrast to traditional borders that are backed up against a hedge or fence and viewed head-on. Plant taller perennials toward the middle of an island bed, then step the heights gradually downward as you get closer to the edges, with the shortest plants framing the bed.

93 **The tallest plant in an island bed should be no more than half the diameter of the bed.** Proportion is important within an island bed. Think of it as a small world of its own, and choose plants that are in good balance with each other. In an island bed that's 10 feet across, a perennial taller than 5 feet will look disproportionately gawky, and there won't be enough room to step down gracefully from such a tall central plant.

94 **To give island beds weight, select a few substantial plants for the center.** Island beds often seem to float in a sea of lawn and can look flimsy compared to neighboring borders. To strengthen them, plant husky perennials toward the center. Choose plants that look good for a long time. Try the finest loosestrife, *Lysimachia ephemerum*, a subtle, columnar plant with dark green leaves and spikes of white flowers. A statuesque ornamental grass such as variegated Japanese silver grass (*Miscanthus sinensis* 'Variegatus') makes an interesting foliage accent toward the middle of an island bed.

Culver's root (*Veronicastrum virginicum*) is also a good candidate. Dark green leaves arranged in whorls around the sturdy stems and spikes of white flowers in midsummer distinguish this handsome perennial (it's best grown in full sun).

95 **In generous island beds, try a flowering shrub toward the middle.** If an island bed is greater than

15 feet wide, there's enough room to include a shrub toward the middle (most shrubs occupy at least five feet of space in all directions). Choose one with a long bloom period and a relaxed shape for the best compatibility with neighboring perennials.

Summersweet (*Clethra alnifolia*), a deciduous shrub, is a good central accent for shade. Upright yet loosely open, five-foot-tall summersweet blooms for weeks in late summer. Its white flower spikes combine well with plumes of pinkish lavender *Astilbe tacquetii* 'Superba'.

In sun or partial shade, six-foot-tall tree mallow makes a colorful centerpiece blooming all summer and fall. The species, *Lavatera thuringiaca*, has deep pink flowers. Named cultivars such as bright pink 'Candy Floss' and light pink 'Barnsley' are gaining popularity. Tree mallows die down nearly to the ground in winter and grow back from the base in spring, much like perennials.

Medium-sized shrub roses also fit well at the center of island beds in sun. Pastel pink 'Penelope', a hybrid musk rose, and deep red 'Scarlet Meidiland', a shrub rose, are excellent choices.

96 To anchor an island bed that seems adrift, add a structural element. A birdbath, sundial, or even a large terra-cotta container can be placed within an island bed to give it more weight. Don't wreck your back lugging these heavy objects from spot to spot in the bed to find the right location. Instead, imagine the possibilities by sticking a bamboo stake in potential places. When you've settled on the best spot, move your birdbath or sundial just once.

97 A small structure covered by a suitable climber can serve as a focal point in an island bed. My generous friend Donna Freeman grows annual morning glory vines from seed and shares them with me. I built a rustic teepee by sticking tall apple branches in the ground at a 45-degree angle and tying them at the top with twine. By midsummer, purple morning glories cover the teepee, making a sensational pyramid at the center of a sunny island bed.

98 In island beds, stay away from perennials that lose their form or become shabby. There's no way to hide sudden gaps in island beds–they're seen from all sides. Goatsbeard (*Aruncus sylvester*), queen-of-the-prairie (*Filipendula rubra*), queen-of-the-meadow (*Filipendula ulmaria*), and foxglove (*Digitalis purpurea*) disappear, for all practical purposes, after their spent blooms are snipped off. This transformation leaves too much dead space in their wake.

Avoid plants such as cardoon and angelica that are bold in spring but go downhill by midsummer. Every plant in an island bed must count.

99 Group several island beds together for a more effective display. One island bed carved out of a lawn looks a little lost, but several look as if they belong together. A trio is very pleasing, and you can relate them to each other by repeating the same color scheme or by planting some of the same perennials in all three island beds.

100 Edge island beds with bricks or flat rocks for a crisp outline. Stone and brick define the shape of a bed with a ribbon of color and texture that separates plants from lawn. Make a shallow, level ditch at the perimeter, top it with a layer of sand, and carefully arrange the hard materials. Fill any gaps with more sand.

101 If you want to emphasize the shape of an island, edge the entire bed with one variety of perennial. When a friend was thinning a colony of *Geranium ibericum*, I used the extras to frame an oval bed, planting them a foot apart all along the perimeter. Every spring for at least eight weeks this island is encircled by deep blue-violet flowers. Lovely lobed leaves that stand a foot tall hold the edge before and after bloom time, unifying the design.

102 For an instant screen, plant an island bed with tall perennials and annuals. Instead of building a fence, let perennials form a green wall. This is effective when you need privacy mainly in summer and fall. Tall beauties such as Michaelmas daisies, sneezeweed (*Helenium autumnale*), Joe-Pye weed (*Eupatorium purpureum*), perennial sunflowers (*Helianthus*), and boltonia are excellent for hedging. To thicken this kind of planting quickly, add annual sunflowers, cosmos, and spider flower (*Cleome*) to the tapestry.

103 Shape your island beds to best serve their function. In the middle of a large lawn, generous oval island beds look graceful. Where I needed a baffle to separate the upper backyard from the wilderness below, a long narrow rectangle was the best shape for maximum screening.

When I got around to developing the lower backyard, I wanted a blaze of long-lasting summer and fall color. I constructed two concentric beds, each crescent shaped, with a path sandwiched in between for strolling. From a distance these two beds merge to appear as one enormous, thickly planted border, just the illusion I wanted to create. Yet the path between them lets you wander along for close-up viewing and makes a good place to kneel and weed.

104 **Make sure your island beds are in good proportion to the overall size of the garden and in balance with each other.** Take a good look at the space that you're designing, and think of it as a large, gracious living room. Your lawn is the equivalent of hardwood floors, your island beds like colorful area rugs. Just as you'd coordinate the size of your carpets, keeping them in scale with each other and the size of the room, make sure the dimensions of your island beds relate well with one another and the overall size of the garden.

When in doubt, err on the side of generosity. I've seen many more gardens suffering from skimpy, inadequate beds than from oversized borders.

105 **Avoid aggressive plants within island beds.** Compatible growth rates are crucial within the confines of an island bed. A delicate balance must be struck between neighbors or else rampant perennials will take over. Island beds are not the place for plants that run slyly underground—stay away from gooseneck loosestrife (*Lysimachia clethroides*), golden loosestrife (*Lysimachia punctata*), Mrs. Robb's spurge (*Euphorbia robbiae*), and G*eranium* 'Claridge Druce'. They belong where a running ground cover is desired—under the canopy of deciduous trees or in the wilder parts of large gardens. Avoid self-sowers as well (feverfew, lady's mantle, forget-me-not) and you will spend less time weeding them out.

106 When island beds are surrounded by lawn, select edging plants with enough height and leaf definition to contrast with the grass. Compact forms of lavender, such as 'Loddon Blue', 'Hidcote', 'Royal Velvet', and Spanish lavender (*Lavandula stoechas pedunculata*) make excellent low hedges to frame an island bed. Tall and stocky enough to keep the turf from invading, their gray leaves offer a welcome transition from green grass. Moonbeam tickseed (*Coreopsis* 'Moonbeam') also forms a low hedge loaded with light yellow flowers all summer long.

Many cranesbills have attractively lobed leaves that are excellent for the front of an island bed. Choose those with moderate growth rates: *Geranium renardii, Geranium nodosum, Geranium cantabrigiense, Geranium sanguineum* 'Album', and *Geranium cinereum* 'Subcaulescens'. For shady island beds, select hostas, coral bells (*Heuchera* hybrids), lungworts (*Pulmonaria* hybrids), rodgersias, and masterworts (*Astrantia major*) for their decorative foliage.

107 When island beds are surrounded by gravel, stone, or concrete, select edging plants that drape gracefully onto the hard surfaces. Although sprawlers are a nuisance overflowing onto a lawn, they're delightful trailing onto a path. Sun roses (*Helianthemum* hybrids) with sprays of red, orange, yellow, pink, or white flowers make splashes of color in early summer. (Give them good drainage to prevent root rot.) Santa Barbara daisies (*Erigeron karvinskianus*) form plump pillows of pink and white flowers that bloom all summer. Trailing cranesbills such as magenta *Geranium* 'Ann Folkard' or *Geranium* x *riversleaianum* 'Russell Pritchard', and soft pink *Geranium* x *riversleaianum* Mavis Simpson' billow and also weave comfortably into nearby plants.

Several herbaceous cinquefoils (*Potentilla* species and hybrids) have trailing flowers. Their attractive strawberry like leaves hold interest before and after the charming clusters of flowers bloom. Enjoy bright red *Potentilla* 'Gibson's Scarlet', pinkish *Potentilla* 'Miss Wilmott', or maroon *Potentilla* 'Etna'.

108 Plant trailing perennials with colored foliage for especially showy accents at the front of island beds that are surrounded by a hard surface (gravel, brick, pavers). Clove-scented pinks (*Dianthus plumarius*) with silvery leaves that glimmer all year long look great where they can freely spill onto a path, wafting fragrance in late spring. Their delicious flowers may be pink ('Inchmery', 'Pike's Pink'), red ("Brympton Red'), white ('Mrs. Sinkins'), or even bicolored ('Laced Romeo', 'Little Jock', 'Pheasant's Eye').

An abundance of trailing sedums offer succulent leaves in many hues. Burgundy-leaved *Sedum spurium* 'Dragon's Blood' has bright pinkish red flowers, *Sedum kamtschaticum* has bright green leaves and yellow flowers, while gray-green *Sedum sieboldii* has pink flowers that bloom surprisingly late in fall.

109 Plant upright perennials with colored foliage for eye-catching accents at the edges of island beds surrounded by lawn. In shade, grow fancy-leaved coral bells (*Heuchera*) such as 'Palace Purple', 'Chocolate Ruffles', 'Ruby Veil', and 'Velvet Night', with delicate spikes of pinkish white flowers rising above their hand-shaped leaves in early summer. *Bergenia* 'Sunningdale', with oxblood winter foliage, red stems, and reddish purple flowers that light up the winter garden, thrives in sun or partial shade.

Several of the sun-loving spurges and upright sedums sport colored foliage. Purple wood spurge (*Euphorbia amygdaloides* 'Rubra') has maroon foliage that is especially pronounced in spring, with contrasting bright yellow flower heads. An even darker spurge, cocoa *Euphorbia dulcis* 'Chameleon', makes a striking accent at the front of an island bed. *Sedum* 'Mohrchen' has succulent burgundy leaves that create a stir when they push up in spring. Upright through most of the summer, 'Mohrchen' has a tendency to sprawl by August and may need some staking as it grows up, or a rock to lean upon.

Perennial Partners for Every Season

‿჻ઽ჻⁀

What Makes a Good Partnership

Matching perennials with each other is like playing three-dimensional chess. For the most colorful garden, keep in mind sequence of bloom, simultaneous bloom, and a balance of flowers for each season. Choose perennials over all four seasons, so that your bloom sequence is year-round, with new flowers coming into bloom just as others are fading. At the same time, focus on planting groups of perennials that bloom together to create seasonal vignettes, rather than scattering the color haphazardly.

For example, instead of dotting the landscape with a lungwort (*Pulmonaria*) here and a daffodil there and a leopard's bane (*Doronicum*) elsewhere, join these three late-winter bloomers in a united group for a stronger composition. Do the same with trios of spring, summer, and fall bloomers, allowing enough color for each season so that you will never suffer from flower deprivation.

111 Keep in mind the horticultural requirements of perennials when choosing suitable partners. Siberian iris, Japanese iris, candelabra primroses (*Primula japonica, Primula pulverulenta*), and calla lilies all enjoy damp soil. Since they thrive in the same environment and bloom in late spring, they're ideal companions.

Similarly tickweed (*Coreopsis*) and 'Lucifer' montbretia love full sun, tolerate heavy clay, and bloom in midsummer in compatible shades of yellow and red. Lavender, purple toadflax (*Linaria purpurea*), and pink evening primrose (*Oenothera speciosa*) make good neighbors–all are tolerant of dry soil and bloom in midsummer.

112 Pair perennials with similar growth rates–they make good neighbors. Daylilies and 'Autumn Joy' sedums both expand at about the same speed, allowing each other equal growth opportunity. Daylilies, peonies, and spiderwort (*Tradescantia virginiana*) also expand at about the same pace. But a slower spreader such as *Alchemilla alpina,* a diminutive form of lady's mantle, should be placed near other small, moderate growers–compact hostas or coral bells. Put it near a daylily or a peony and it will soon get swallowed up.

113 Contrast opposite colors, textures, and forms to create the most dramatic combinations. Purple and yellow, blue and orange set up an electric tension that makes both colors in the pair appear more vibrant. Juxtaposing crepe-papery poppies with woolly lamb's ears or prickly globe thistle with feathery queen-of-the-prairie makes each texture more visible and remarkable. Contrasting delphinium spikes with peony globes and astilbe plumes with lacy meadow rue makes each flower shape an arresting foil for its opposite.

Winter Partners

114 Treat yourself to winter compositions for early cheer. White Christmas roses (*Helleborus niger*) and pink Lenten roses (*Helleborus orientalis*) are the first perennials to bloom in my garden. Their nodding, bell-shaped flowers are studded with golden stamens. I like pairing them with blue, pink, and white lungworts (*Pulmonaria* species and hybrids). Hellebores' handsome, hand-shaped leaves are deep green and glossy, while lungworts' spoon-shaped foliage is soft as felt. *Pulmonaria longifolia* and *Pulmonaria saccharata* have silver-splashed leaves, while the leaves of *Pulmonaria angustifolia* are solid green. Hellebores and lungworts both prefer shade.

115 Brighten woodland floors with colorful winter blooms. Searching for a low-growing carpet beneath deciduous trees or beside a woodland path? Try liverwort (*Hepatica americana*), with single flowers in shades of pink and blue-violet. Add magenta- and white-flowering winter cyclamen (*Cyclamen coum*) and drifts of purple julianna primrose (*Primula juliae* and its hybrids). I much prefer the dainty-leaved juliannas, which blend easily into beds and borders before and after bloom time, to the polyantha primroses with distracting, coarser leaves. Winter-flowering cyclamen springs from a tough underground corm that is drought tolerant enough to survive at the base of big trees.

116 Plant winter-blooming bulbs to broaden your color palette. Early snowdrops (*Galanthus nivalis*) add a sparkle of white to winter compositions. Dainty and graceful, they're best enjoyed in groups of fifteen or more. Plenty of daffodils flower in February and March. 'Tête-à-Tête', 'Jack Snipe', 'February Gold', and 'Minnow' offer long-lasting flowers that brighten the early garden, harbingers of the tulips and daffodils that arrive later in spring.

Spring Partners

117 Match partners that enhance each other for spring vignettes. Luscious peony flowers benefit from the company of subtler cranesbills. Try 'Red Charm' peonies with an underpinning of blue-violet *Geranium himalayense*, or pink 'Sarah Bernhardt' peonies with a skirt of white *Geranium sanguineum* 'Striatum'.

Vertical spikes of pink and cream foxgloves complement the purple and blue flowers of Siberian iris toward the back of a border. Deliciously fragrant lemon lily (*Hemerocallis lilioasphodelus*), the earliest daylily to bloom, pairs well with blue-violet *Geranium pratense* or blue flax (*Linum perenne*).

Bright yellow spurges need equally intense partners for a good balance. Try cushion spurge (*Euphorbia poly-*

chroma) with purple dwarf bearded iris, or the taller *Euphorbia palustris* with purple 'Caesar's Brother' Siberian iris. Red or orange tulips would also flatter the golden spurges. Just remember that tulips like it dry in the summer.

Summer Partners

118 Keep the color going all summer with compatible long-blooming companions. For longest-lasting color from summer through fall, try a trio of blue Frikart's asters (*Aster* x *frikartii*), white *Gaura lindheimerii,* and purple coneflowers (*Echinacea purpurea*). The sizable coneflowers and asters will stand out against a cloud of profuse-flowering *Gaura,* which *looks* as delicate as baby's breath but is actually tough enough to flourish in clay soil.

For a subtle, romantic picture, place pink evening primrose (*Oenothera speciosa*) behind a hedge of 'Grosso' lavender. The round pink flowers juxtapose well with vertical, fragrant spikes of lavender. Both plants are sun lovers and drought tolerant.

119 Plant plenty of phlox and mallow for midsummer. Fragrant summer phlox (*Phlox paniculata*) marries well with the mallows (*Malva fastigiata*). Both bloom in shades of pink and white, the phloxes with rounded flowers at the top of tall stems, the mallows in long-lasting spikes. Larger tree mallow (*Lavatera thuringiaca*) swells to shrub size by midsummer, full of hibiscus-shaped flowers. Blend it with white goose-goes-walking (*Lysimachia clethroides*) and lavender Russian sage (*Perovskia atriplicifolia*).

Some of the summer phloxes, such as electric pink-red 'Starfire' and salmon-pink 'Sir John Falstaff', need equally bright companions. 'White Swan' coneflower works well, or the brilliant blue flowers of half-hardy *Salvia patens*.

120 When it's hot out, let the colors sizzle too. It's hard to beat the tickweeds for vigor and long bloom period—bright yellow threadleaf tickweed (*Coreopsis verticillata*) and buttery *Coreopsis* 'Moonbeam'. Both look great with red-orange 'Lucifer' montbretia (*Crocosmia* 'Lucifer') and red daylilies. For more fire, add red-orange blanketflower (*Gaillardia grandiflora*), red yarrow (*Achillea* 'Paprika'), and golden yarrow (*Achillea* 'Coronation Gold').

121 Don't miss a beat in late summer—let the *Rudbeckia* tribe keep the color going strong. A strong surge of color begins in August with bright yellow Rudbeckia 'Goldsturm', bearing three-foot-tall black-eyed Susans on strong stems. Not much later, four-foot-tall *Rudbeckia triloba* comes along, a veritable shrub full of smaller yellow flowers, each with a distinctive dark center. Gigantic *Rudbeckia nitida* towers at the back of borders in the company of sunflowers and lavender Joe-Pye weed (*Eupatorium purpureum*). Its drooping yellow flowers have greenish cones that point to the sky. The double form of yellow coneflower, 'Goldquelle', looks a lot like a dahlia.

Fall Partners

122 **Extend the season by choosing partners that bloom in the fall.** Obedient plant (*Physostegia virginiana*) begins flowering in late summer and continues into autumn, with pink or white spikes. I like pink 'Carmen' sedum in front of the white form of obedient plant (*Physostegia virginiana* 'Alba'), and white 'Stardust' sedum in front of the pink forms of obedient plant.

Tall Michaelmas daisies are faithful bloomers in fall–blue, pink, and white daisies smother their branches for weeks. Add sneezeweed (*Helenium autumnale*), a medium-height beauty with yellow ray flowers, or white boltonia (*Boltonia asteroides*) to complete the picture.

123 **Pair ornamental grasses and se-dums for striking fall composi-tions.** Ornamental grasses flower in late summer and fall. I'm partial to 'Rehbraun' red switchgrass (*Panicum virgatum* 'Rehbraun'), with filmy spikes of red flowers. Place this linear grass behind a succulent clump of 'Stardust' sedum for contrast of form and texture. 'Red Baron' bloodgrass (*Imperata cylindrica* 'Red Baron') pleases me too. Its upright red leaves are smashing be-side the round, blue-green leaves of draping Siebold's sedum (*Sedum sieboldiana*).

Striped zebra grass (*Miscanthus sinensis* 'Zebrinus') combines well with 'Autumn Joy' sedum–both are vigorous growers with distinctive character. Blue oat grass (*Helictotrichon sempervirens*), refined and cooling, is a good partner for draping 'Vera Jameson' sedum, with exotic grayish purple leaves.

124 **Plant ironweed (*Vernonia nove-boracensis*) and Maximilian sunflower (*Helianthus maximilianii*) for a wild meadow look in your fall garden.** Ironweed's six-foot-tall strong stems are topped by clusters of flowers that resemble asters. In my garden it grows happily in full sun in clay-based soil, in the company of perennial sunflowers, asters, Joe-Pye weed (*Eupa-torium purpureum*), and fall-flowering sedums.

Maximilian sunflower is a novel surprise that I look forward to every fall. It gets so tall (at least eight feet) that it winds itself into a nearby pear tree. Dozens of bright yellow-rayed blooms open from bottom to top along amazingly wiggly yet sturdy stems. Every stem telescopes, rising taller and taller, opening flower bud after flower bud, as if to say fall will never end.

Combining Perennials that Bloom in Different Seasons

125 **Combine perennials that bloom in different seasons, and skip the worry about clashing flowers.** Some perennials have leaves that are even more interesting than their flowers, and you may want to think about their foliage first when choosing compatible companions. 'Red Baron' bloodgrass (*Imperata cylindrica* 'Red Baron') has bright red leaves that contrast attractively with bergenia's (*Bergenia cordifolia*) green, ear-shaped leaves. Fortunately the bergenia's magenta-pink flowers bloom in winter, well before the new leaves of bloodgrass have emerged.

The flowers of 'Autumn Joy' sedum are an orange-pink that clash with many of the pink flowers in the fall garden. By combining it with Lenten rose

(*Helleborus orientalis*), which blooms pink in winter, the charm is in the contrast of the sedum's succulent, gray-green leaves with the hand-shaped, dark green foliage of the hellebore.

126 **Plant perennials together that can support each other.** Lenten rose is good company for *Kirengeshoma palmata*, a perennial with handsome maple-like foliage and tubular yellow flowers in autumn that has the unfortunate habit of flopping forward at bloom time. I place it behind the Lenten rose, allowing it to lean on the hellebore instead of falling flat on its face.

127 **Where it's hot and dry, plant pinks and sedums for great foliage tapestries.** In sunny dry places mix cottage pinks (*Dianthus plumarius*) and 'Ruby Glow' sedums. The cottage pinks have gray foliage and an array of pink, white, or wine-colored flowers in spring, while the dark, succulent-leaved sedums offer pinkish burgundy flowers in fall. Foliage color contrast and textural contrast make these two plants good partners for three seasons, even though they don't bloom together.

128 **In dry shade, take advantage of hardy cranesbills and hardy cy-**

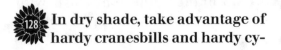

clamen. *Geranium macrorrhizum,* a cranesbill with lobed leaves that stay evergreen year-round, and magenta flowers that bloom in spring to early summer, is resilient in dry shade. Similarly, fall-blooming cyclamen (*Cyclamen hederifolium*) can put up with shade and little water. Its round, silvery leaves are lovely alone and a good contrast to the lobed green cranesbill foliage. The equally beautiful winter-blooming *Cyclamen coum* comes in white and magenta cultivars.

By planting several forms of *Geranium macrorrhizum,* say rosy red 'Bevan's Variety', clear light pink 'Ingwersen's Variety', and blush-pink *Geranium macrorrhizum* 'Album', with both pink and white forms of winter- and fall-blooming hardy cyclamen, tons of color can be enjoyed through three seasons, along with gorgeous leaves.

Perennials for Many Purposes

Fragrant Perennials

129 Choose fragrant perennials to create a romantic atmosphere in your shade garden. Scent is remembered far longer than sight, sound, taste, or touch, registering deep down in our consciousness. The fragrance of lilacs or lilies often evokes remembrances of grandmother's garden or a trip to the country in childhood.

Lily-of-the-valley's sweet perfume wafts through the shady understory, blending with that of delicate-blooming sweet woodruff. Both perennials are rompers and should only be planted where they won't smother shyer plants.

Each blooms white, sweet woodruff a lace of tiny flowers, lily-of-the-valley a petite spike of dainty bells. Sweet cicely (*Myrrhis odorata*), also a shade lover, has ferny leaves that taste like anise and fragrant white flowers resembling Queen Anne's lace. The dark seedpods have a licorice flavor and make a lovely textural accent in the border–they self-sow, and you may want to prevent this by deadheading.

130 Plant plenty of scented perennials in sunny borders. Many of the bearded iris have fragrance. I have a pass-along purple one that smells just like ripe grapes and a bronze one that smells like root beer. I adore the little plum tart iris (*Iris gramineus*), elegantly shaped with a fruity scent.

Tall white valerian (*Valeriana officinalis*) reminds me of vanilla, while many of the oriental lilies and cottage pinks (*Dianthus plumarius*) have a clovelike perfume. Selected peonies such as white 'Louise Marx', white 'Walter Marx', pink 'Mrs. Franklin D. Roosevelt', and red 'Big Ben' are prized for their fragrance. When it comes to scented daylilies, 'Hyperion', with large yellow trumpets, 'Frank Hunter', a creamy yellow with ruffled petals, and yellow 'So Sweet' are among my favorites.

131 Add herbal perennials to your sunny borders for scent and drought tolerance. Lavender makes an excellent front-of-the-border plant, with gray foliage that offers good contrast to green grass. Its flower spikes in shades of purple, pink, and white waft fragrance all summer long. Lavender also attracts bees and butterflies.

I love 'Arp' rosemary for its dark green, upright stems and tiny pastel blue flowers that bloom as early as February in a mild winter. Pinch the needle-like leaves to release a sweet, minty scent, so refreshing on a hot summer day.

Most flowering thymes are aromatic and make low-growing ground covers in sunny places, provided there's good drainage. I love lemon thyme's (*Thymus* x *citriodorus*) deliciously lemon-scented foliage. 'Gold Edge' lemon thyme has the added value of a gold rim to each green leaf, while 'Silver Queen' lemon thyme has gray-green leaves edged with white.

Perennials for Bouquets

132 Make sure to have plenty of showy flowers to cut for bouquets. How luxurious to freely snip blossoms for the house and enjoy the details of their beauty close up! Peonies, irises, lilies, kaffir lilies (*Schizostylis coccinea*), summer phlox, coneflowers

(*Echinacea purpurea*), pincushion flowers (*Scabiosa caucasica*), speedwells, bellflowers (*Campanula*), delphiniums, Frikart's asters, gooseneck loosestrifes (*Lysimachia clethroides*), fringed loosestrifes (*Lysimachia ciliata*), Peruvian lilies (*Alstroemeria aurantiaca*), three-lobed coneflowers (*Rudbeckia triloba*), black-eyed Susans (*Rudbeckia* 'Goldsturm'), and tickseeds (*Coreopsis grandiflora*) are excellent choices for cutting.

133 Be sure to grow small-flowering perennials to use as filler in arrangements. Baby's breath, feverfew, white yarrow (*Achillea decolorans* 'W. B. Child'), *Aster ericoides, Asteromoea mongolica,* and *Gaura lindheimerii* have dainty white flowers that knit the larger blooms together. Yellow pincushion flower (*Scabiosa ochroleuca*) and lady's mantle (*Alchemilla mollis*) have delicate yellow flowers that are useful in warm-toned bouquets or to liven up the cool blues. Meadow rue has misty flowers in lavender, white, and yellow, airy as baby's breath. *Calamintha nepetoides* also offers sprays of tiny lavender flowers for bouquets.

Try some ornamental grass flowers in arrangements for a subtle vertical touch—I like the airy flower spikes of red switchgrass (*Panicum virgatum* 'Rehbraun') with burgundy dahlias and annual chocolate cosmos.

134 Cut interesting perennial foliage to add pizazz to bouquets. Silvery artemisias such as 'Powys Castle', 'Valerie Finnis', and 'Huntington' make summer and fall flower arrangements shimmer. I find gray especially flattering to red or pink flowers–try 'Powys Castle' with 'Lucifer' montbretia, or 'Huntington' with pink mallows.

Enrich warm-toned bouquets with stems of feathery bronze fennel. Its cocoa-colored foliage is marvelous with orange and yellow montbretias and pokers. Use blades of variegated ornamental grass or variegated sweet flag to create color echoes with white or yellow flowers in a bouquet. Introduce bold oval leaves of bergenia, arum, calla lily, or hosta to anchor a flower arrangement.

Use your imagination and try out new effects. A few stems of variegated boxwood, a couple of trailing stems of grape vine or clematis can add unexpected charm to an ordinary bouquet.

Perennials for Containers

135 Keep a few tiny vases around for the dainty flowers that are easily overlooked in the great outdoors. I like to pick handfuls of the early grape hyacinths and bouquets of spring-flowering cottage pinks, the better to appreciate the grace and fragrance of these small treasures. Species tulips (*Tulipa tarda, Tulipa clusiana*) and delicate rock garden daffodils ('Hawera', 'Minnow') that would be lost in a bigger arrangement are delightful in a dainty cream pitcher or a recycled spice jar.

My neighbor Gavin Younie once brought me a green caper jar filled with red nasturtiums that lasted the better part of a week on my kitchen counter. Capers have now become part of my cuisine, mainly for the slender green jars that are the perfect size for mini bouquets.

136 To make bouquets last longest, cut flowers when it's cool out and practice good sanitation. The best time to cut flowers is late in the evening or early in the morning–heat stresses flowers. Strip off all lower leaves so that they won't rot in the water, and crush or slit any stems that are woody. Plunge the flowers into a bucket of cold water, arranging them loosely for good air circulation. Store your flowers for several hours in a cool place such as a basement to condition them.

When you're ready to arrange your bouquets, recut the stems, and slit or crush the woody ones again too. If you display them in the cooler parts of your house, away from direct sunshine, the flowers will last longer.

137 Improve your containers by adding perennials with long bloom periods to the compositions. Perennials expand the color and textural choices when added to pots of annuals. Select those that are self-supporting to avoid unsightly stakes. Blue flax (*Linum perenne*), with fine foliage and pleasing sky blue flowers in spring, and 'Moonbeam' tickseed, loaded with yellow flowers all summer, both combine well with annuals.

Spikes of beardtongue (*Penstemon* hybrids) such as red 'Firebird', purple 'Midnight Blue', burgundy 'Garnet', and 'Elfin Pink' make good central plantings, accompanied by annuals such as trailing verbena or blue swan river daisy billowing out at the edges of the pot. Russian sage (*Perovskia atriplicifolia*), with spikes of lavender flowers in late summer and fall, and blue oat grass (*Helictotrichon sempervirens*), both form attractive upright accents in containers.

138 Enjoy the beauty of rampant perennials in containers where their aggressive nature is safely held in check. Although chameleon plant (*Houttuynia cordata* 'Variegata') is prized for its showy leaves that are marbled green, red, and yellow, it can easily take over a bed, especially in damp soil. Instead, let it fill a pot and spill over the edges.

Variegated yellow archangel (*Lamium galeobdolon* 'Variegatum') has attractive heart-shaped green leaves marked with silver. Unfortunately, it spreads rapidly by surface runners that root down at the nodes. Avoid this headache by planting it in a container placed in a shady area where the silvery leaves will introduce light.

Perennials for Screening

139 **Plant tall perennials where you need screening in summer and fall.** For summer privacy near sitting areas and patios, perennials can do the job faster and more economically than trees and shrubs. Tree mallows (*Lavatera thuringiaca*, *Lavatera* 'Barnsley', 'Candy Floss', 'Burgundy') full of summer flowers in shades of pink and burgundy will rise six feet in their second season—so will Joe-Pye weed (*Eupatorium giganteum*), with large lavender flower heads in late summer, and giant Chinese silver grass (*Miscanthus floridulus*), which sends up creamy plumes in fall.

Perennials with Especially Long Bloom Periods

140 **Take advantage of perennials with long blooming periods to**

maximize color in your garden. For winter and early spring, Lenten roses (*Helleborus orientalis*) and lungwort *(Pulmonaria longifolia, P. saccharata, P. angustifolia)* provide months of color. Several of spring's cranesbills flower for six weeks and more: pink *Geranium sanguineum* 'Striatum' and blue *Geranium ibericum* head my list.

Many of summer's cranesbills are also long bloomers–if you love magenta, plant *Geranium sanguineum* 'Cedric Morris' or *Geranium psilostemon.* Purple coneflowers (*Echinacea purpurea*) and blue asters (*Aster* x *frikartii*) bloom for months on end–so do the threadleaf tickseeds (*Coreopsis verticillata, Coreopsis* 'Zagreb', *Coreopsis* 'Moonbeam'), white *Gaura lindheimerii,* and Russian sage *(Perovskia atriplicifolia).* Blanket flower (*Gaillardia grandiflora*), beardtongue (*Penstemon* hybrids), and perennial pincushion flower (*Scabiosa caucasica*) also bloom all summer and fall if deadheaded.

Fall's kaffir lily (*Schizostylis coccinea*) and obedience plant (*Physostegia virginiana*) are faithful bloomers for a good eight weeks. Each of these has cultivars in several shades of pink and white, adding to our autumn pleasure.

 141 **To attract wonderful butterflies, plant plenty of blue-violet and**

lavender-pink perennials. 'Bowles Mauve' wallflower (*Erysimum* 'Bowles Mauve') draws the early butterflies in spring and keeps luring them all summer. My 'Grosso' lavender hedge attracts butterflies like crazy. So does a stand of old-fashioned, fragrant summer phlox (*Phlox paniculata*). Butterflies dance among the purple coneflowers (*Echinacea purpurea*) and at the tops of *Stachys macrantha*'s lavender flower spikes. They flock to pink autumn-flowering sedums (*Sedum spectabile*) and purple *Verbena bonariensis* and to fall-flowering dwarf asters and the late yellow coneflower *Rudbeckia nitida*.

If a flower is tubular and orange, the hummingbirds will find it. Every summer hummingbirds blitz the back borders where red-orange *Crocosmia* 'Lucifer' blazes away. They plunder the orange butterfly weed (*Asclepias tuberosa*) and zip in and out of montbretia spikes (*Crocosmia crocosmiflora*). They visit red-hot poker and beardtongue, bee balm, honeysuckle, fuchsia, California fuchsia (*Zauschneria californica*), and cape fuchsia (*Phygelius capensis*).

Perennials for Challenging Places

Dry Shade

143 **Skip the bark dust—plenty of tough perennials put up with dry shade.** I rely on stalwart perennials to liven up areas beneath old trees. Bishop's hat (*Epimedium* x *versicolor)* is a favorite for its heart-shaped evergreen leaves. Small, columbine-like yellow flowers bloom in early spring. *Epimedium* x *rubrum,* with reddish pink flowers, is slower to spread but has the added charm of burgundy tones in the new leaves.

Several cranesbills tolerate dry shade and make excellent ground covers. Evergreen *Geranium macrorrhizum* is the most vigorous, with lobed leaves and magenta spring flowers. The bloody cranesbill (*Geranium sanguineum*) will grow vigorously in sunny areas and moderately in dry shade—its hot pink flowers bloom for most of the summer above daintily dissected leaves. *Geranium* x *cantabrigiense* 'Biokovo' also grows well in dry shade. Its small, lobed leaves are topped by blush-pink flowers that appear in late spring and early summer.

Hardy cyclamen that bloom in winter (*Cyclamen coum*) and in fall (*Cyclamen hederifolium*) are drought tolerant and prefer shade. Their white and hot pink flowers are as showy as their rounded leaves that are marbled with silver.

144 When searching for perennials for dry shade, consider plants that are nearly weeds in normal situations. Mrs. Robb's spurge (*Euphorbia robbiae*) has a domineering nature and will quickly smother other more polite perennials in a border. But where there's plenty of room, say at the base of an old apple tree, it's terrific. Dark green rosettes that look polished decorate the ground in winter and send up stems of bright yellow flowers that bloom in spring.

Similarly aggressive, bearsfoot hellebore (*Helleborus foetidus*) can be a nuisance in rich soil, self-sowing like crazy. In dry shade, it's great. Evergreen foliage and greenish-yellow winter flowers rimmed with a fine red edge make it an outstanding perennial.

I've ripped cartloads of golden loose-strife (*Lysimachia punctata*) out of perennial borders, but saved some starts for the dry shady bed near my neighbor's greedy laurel hedge. The loosestrife carries on with little water in dense shade; yellow flower spikes bloom in early summer. I let Labrador viola (*Viola labradorica*) have its way in this area too. A pesty spreader by rhizome and seed elsewhere in the garden, in dry shade it's a great filler, thriving where less intrepid plants shrivel. Its dark purplish black leaves and purple flowers are delightful.

Heavy Clay

145 **Heavy clay soil requires amending with compost in the long haul, but until you've accomplished that daunting task, plant perennials that can survive.** Ideally we prepare the soil first and plant later, but it's hard to postpone joy, especially if you have a big garden where soil preparation can take years. Meanwhile, try some clay-tolerant perennials to cheer you on.

Daylilies are the toughest plants in my garden, spreading and blooming despite heavy clay that's only been only slightly amended with compost. So are Siberian iris–they thrive on neglect. My only complaint is having to divide the enormous clumps every few years with an ax.

Autumn-flowering sedums (*Sedum spectabile*) flourish anywhere and everywhere in my garden, including areas of wet clay soil, dry and hot places, even in shade. With so many cultivars to choose from ('Carmen', 'Meteor', 'Brilliant', 'Stardust', 'Autumn Joy') you can enjoy many shades of pink and white.

Geranium endressii, the pink-flowering cranesbill that blooms all summer, and *Geranium pratense*, with blue flowers in spring, have also flourished in clay soil. Be aware, however, that both are vigorous spreaders and that *Geranium pratense* is prone to powdery mildew in very wet seasons.

Asteromoea mongolica, a clump-forming perennial that blooms nearly all summer with small, asterlike white flowers, puts up with clay and drought. Purple toadflax (*Linaria purpurea*) will also grow just about anywhere in any kind of soil. I get tired of weeding out the extra seedlings, but the lavender spikes of flowers that bloom for weeks in the summer make the job worth the effort.

Gooseneck loosestrife (*Lysimachia clethroides*) and golden loosestrife (*Lysimachia punctata*) are both tolerant of clay. Like most of the perennials I'm listing here, they'll spread much faster in looser soil than in packed clay.

Boggy Beds

146 **Choose from the many species of water-loving iris to fill boggy beds.** Yellow flag iris (*Iris pseudacorus*) is probably the most common inhabitant of marshy ground but is suitable for large expanses only–it spreads vigorously by root and seed. Bright yellow flowers herald early summer, blooming freely at the edges of ponds where it's damp and even in standing water. In my garden, the variegated form (*Iris pseudacorus* 'Variegata') and named cultivars such as *Iris pseudacorus* 'Holden Clough' and *I. p.* 'Roy Davidson' have been less aggressive and safer in beds and borders. I've exiled the standard yellow flag iris to the drainage ditches at the edges of the garden where they can revel freely in the moisture.

Siberian iris also love damp soil. Growing in grassy clumps with purple, pink, blue, and white flowers in early summer, they swell outward to form larger and larger stands and must be divided every few years for the best flower production. When left to burgeon on their own for too long they get so massive that you'll need a work party with several spades to lift and divide them.

Elegant Japanese iris (*Iris ensata*) have large flowers that seem to hover above the stems like oversized butterflies. Their color range is plentiful –purple, magenta, white, pink, blue, and striped forms abound. One blossom floating in a bowl is enough to make my day.

The blue flag iris (*Iris versicolor*) is also a beauty, especially 'Gerald Darby', with striking black stems and violet flowers. Louisiana iris thrive in damp borders, offering velvety flowers in shades of purple, white, yellow, and reddish purple. Spuria iris, among the tallest (five feet and more) are also latest to bloom (July) with sizable yellow, lavender, white, purple, and even magenta flowers.

147 Sweet flag and obedience plant are also great perennials for wet places. Sweet flag is a grassy perennial that loves marshy soil. I find the variegated form, *Acorus calamus* 'Variegatus', most satisfying. Irislike blades striped green and creamy yellow make a striking accent in a border, near the edges of a pond, or even rising up through shallow water. This perennial creeps by rhizomes but it is easy to dig out any extras.

Obedient plant (*Physostegia virgin-*

iana) also thrives in damp borders, with pink or white flower spikes coloring up in late summer and fall. Pink-flowering forms run more freely and bloom longer in my garden than the white form.

148 **Plant rodgersias, astilbes, and masterworts to brighten damp shade.** Relieve the darkness by choosing pastel flowers and elegant foliage to enhance shady places. Where it's damp, rodgersia will flourish. Fingerleaf rodgersia (*Rodgersia aesculifolia*), with striking leaves resembling horse-chestnut, has creamy white plumes in spring, while 'Superba' featherleaf rodgersia (*Rodgersia pinnata* 'Superba') has pink plumes atop bronze leaves. Dramatic shieldleaf rodgersia (*Rodgersia tabularis*) has big round leaves like bright green frisbees, with nodding, creamy white flower plumes that rise a surprising three feet.

Fernlike leaves and plume-shaped flowers make astilbes the most graceful denizens of damp shade gardens. Choose from pink, peach, white, red, and even lavender varieties. Astilbes contrast well with bolder-leaved hostas and ligularias and blend nicely with lacy ferns and meadow rue.

Masterwort's (*Astrantia major*) lobed leaves emerge bright green in late winter and stay attractive until hard frost. Throughout the summer and fall, fragrant ivory flowers reminiscent of old lace bloom in surges. Let a few flowers age, and scatter the seed that forms nearby to increase your population—masterwort germinates readily this way. Deadhead the majority of flowers to keep the plant in bloom.

Narrow Places

149 Take advantage of narrow beds to contain aggressive plants. Many attractive perennials such as bearded iris, gooseneck loosestrife (*Lysimachia clethroides*), ribbon grass (*Phalaris arundinacea*), and cypress spurge (*Euphorbia cyparissias*) spread vigorously from roots or rhizomes. A narrow bed between the house and a sidewalk is perfect for containing these kinds of rampant growers.

Don't make the mistake of planting creepers strong enough to travel *under* sidewalks—running forms of bamboo and harlequin glory bower tree (*Clerodendrum trichotomum*) will simply slither underground and emerge happily on the other side.

150 Plant plenty of slender, upright perennials in narrow places. Small beds up against fences or walls need tall plants that don't get too wide.

In full sun, try the white-flowering loose-strife, *Lysimachia ephemerum*, with dark green leaves hinting of gray and elegant spikes of white summer flowers. Variegated Japanese silver grass (*Miscanthus sinensis* 'Variegatus'), striped giant reed (*Arundo donax* 'Variegata'), and zebra grass (*Miscanthus sinensis* 'Zebrinus') provide upright striped foliage. For a dainty touch, plant angel's fishing rods, also called fisherman's wands (*Dierama pulcherrimum*), with grassy leaves and sprays of pendant pink flowers that sway gracefully at the tips of long stems.

In shade, foxgloves are slender yet striking. Common foxglove (*Digitalis purpurea*), with furry leaves, blooms with showy spikes of purple or cream. Rusty foxglove (*Digitalis ferruginea*) starts out as an intriguing rosette of strap-shaped leaves at ground level and expands upward capped with spikes of distinctive pale yellow-orange flowers. Yellow fanciers will appreciate straw foxglove (*Digitalis lutea*) and yellow foxglove (*Digitalis grandiflora, Digitalis ambigua*).

Ligularia 'The Rocket' is another good plant for narrow borders in the shade. Handsome arrow-shaped leaves with toothed margins are topped by yellow fireworks in summer.

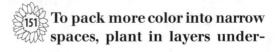 **151 To pack more color into narrow spaces, plant in layers under-**

ground. By mingling bulbs and perennials at different depths you can prolong the sequence of bloom in a small space. Plant the biggest bulbs six to eight inches underground–perhaps 'Pink Perfection' trumpet lilies or purple flowering onions (*Allium* 'Purple Sensation'). At the four-to-six-inch depth, intersperse some daffodils and hyacinths. Closest to ground level, about two inches from the top, add the smallest bulbs–snowdrops, crocus, and netted iris (*Iris reticulata*), which will be first to bloom.

Plant your bulbs in ample groups, and leave space between each group for perennials such as hardy geraniums, summer asters, and balloon flowers that leaf out and bloom later on. These perennials will extend the color even further and also camouflage the yellowing foliage of the bulbs.

Banks and Slopes

152 **Banks are harder on the gardener than on the plants–consider terracing steep places for your own ease.** Aside from one gardener I know who swings around her steep site on ropes, very few of us enjoy being mountain goats. An inhospitable bank can be turned into an inviting garden by reshaping the ground into a series of terraces where you can garden comfortably.

Walls of stone, concrete, or timbers will be needed to retain the soil. When designed with care, these structures add beauty to the garden. I love stone walls—their rugged surfaces form the perfect backdrop for a tapestry of draping perennials. When capped, stone walls also provide a useful surface for sitting and weeding or just plain sitting.

153 **Cover a bank with a fabric barrier before planting to prevent erosion and reduce weeds.** A steep bank is vulnerable to soil erosion from heavy rain and wind. Eventually mature plants root down and anchor the soil, but at planting time a little help from blanketing materials will keep the bank intact and slow down weed germination until the plants have filled out.

Mesh netting made of jute or hemp is available in six-foot-wide rolls. Permeable to water and air, it keeps the soil from sliding downhill. It's easy to plant small perennials in the spaces between the netting grid—for larger plants, cut away some of the mesh to create substantial planting pockets. Add fertilizer at planting time just as you would under ordinary circumstances. Tack the netting firmly in place with U-shaped companion pins. Eventually the netting will decompose—by that time your plants will have matured enough to cover the ground.

Weed barrier made of polyurethane is also available to hold steep banks. Like mesh netting, it's permeable to water and air, but it's a dark color and will take longer to break down, eventually fraying. Holes must be cut for planting pockets since the weave is tight. This material is more suitable for smaller numbers of large bushy perennials and shrubs than for hundreds of perennials on a bank.

154 Perennials that billow and drape are ideal covers for banks. Bare ground is an invitation for weeds to sneak in, so the best plants for banks are those that travel quickly and spread enough to fully occupy all the open space, leaving no room for competition. Artemisia 'Powys Castle' is a good choice for a sunny bank, growing to the size of medium shrub, about three feet wide and equally tall. *Aster* x *frikartii*, loaded with blue daisies all summer, is great too. Bold 'Autumn Joy' sedums are also strong growers–their succulent leaves cover thick stems topped with umbrellas of pinkish flowers in fall.

Mounding perennials such as sunroses (*Helianthemum* hybrids) and Santa Barbara daisies (*Erigeron karvinskianus*) are lovely spilling down a bank or trailing over a low stone wall.

Many of the cranesbills can also serve this purpose–pink-flowering *Geranium* 'Mavis Simpson' and magenta *Geranium* 'Russell Prichard' are among the best.

155 **Choose low-maintenance perennials for steep places–ones that look good from a distance but don't need a lot of fussing.** Choose perennials that only need an annual haircut after their bloom period–for example, lavender, Russian sage (*Perovskia atriplicifolia*), or *Coreopsis* 'Moonbeam', which keep their color all summer and fall without any need for deadheading. Stay away from perennials such as daylilies or *Coreopsis grandiflora* that need frequent grooming to look good–you won't want to scramble up and down a hillside often.

Crevice Plants for Walls and Patios

156 **Leave room in patios for crevice plants to add a decorative touch and release fragrance underfoot.** If you make your patio of stone or brick, add some low-growing perennials for embellishment. Fragrant pinks (*Dianthus plumarius, Dianthus superbus*) add color and scent at ground level. Lemon thyme, chamomile, and Corsican mint send refreshing aromas into the air when crushed underfoot. Dainty julianna primroses (*Primula juliae*) and thrift (*Armeria maritima*) are short enough to decorate small spaces in a paved floor without being obtrusive.

157 Take advantage of stone walls with crevices to display draping perennials. A large expanse of stone-work can be too harsh for a garden, reminiscent of a cemetery. Soften the hard surfaces with trailers that thrive in small pockets. All you need is a bucket of damp soil, a trowel, and enough starter plants to decorate the wall without hiding it. Fill the crevices with good soil and plant your perennials, fitting them tightly into the spaces so that they are well anchored. Don't be afraid to use a firm hand to lodge the plants into their new homes–you want them to be snug.

Smidgens tuck easiest into nooks and crannies. I once planted a client's large stone wall with tiny nibbles from established plants. First I sliced strips off the edges of carpets of thymes, sedums, and campanulas and then divided them into even smaller plugs, about an inch wide. I set these into openings in the wall, as well as in the beds at the top and base of the wall, in autumn. By the following spring, ribbons of color cascaded grace fully against the gray rocks.

Try the trailing bellflowers–*Campanula carpatica* and *Campanula muralis* are both lovely, with blue or white flowers. I like *Geranium* 'Mavis Simpson', with a froth of pink flowers in summer, and lavender *Penstemon campanulatus.* Many succulent-leaved sedums and some spurges (*Euphorbia*) are excellent for textural interest, especially in sunny walls–*Sedum sieboldii*; *Sedum* 'Vera Jameson', 'Ruby Glow', and 'Rosy Glow'; and donkeytail spurge (*Euphorbia palustris*) are favorites. Rock roses (*Helianthemum* hybrids) with billowing masses of pink, yellow, red, white, or orange flowers bring a gray stone wall to life.

158 **Mimic nature by decorating rugged rock walls with the same kind of colorful perennials that grow on rocky cliffsides.** Yellow, orange, red, and purple wallflowers (*Erysimum cheirii, Cheiranthus cheirii, Erysimum* 'Bowles Mauve') make billowing mounds of color that are especially effective when nestled between boulder-sized rocks. Jupiter's beard (*Centranthus ruber*), although often dismissed as a common weed, is useful to soften a harsh stone wall. Its ability to self-sow and survive in the wild without any tending makes it invaluable in places where you don't want to fuss with watering or deadheading.

Maintenance

Staking and Supporting

159 **Stake your floppy perennials with prunings from fruit trees and shrubs.** The easiest and most economical way to support perennials that tend to sprawl–peonies, spiderwort, and chrysanthemums to name just a few–is with woody branches pruned off old fruit trees and overgrown bushes. Choose branches that are sturdy, and cut off the lower side stems to form a stake with a straight lower portion that resembles a tree trunk and upper side branches that look like tree limbs. Ram several of these branches securely into the ground toward the edges of the perennial clump. The outstretched side branches will support the perennials as they grow taller and keep them from flopping downward.

160 Use individual vertical stakes to support tall, narrow flower stems that are likely to break from the weight of the fully developed blooms. Some lilies and most delphiniums are too heavy to hold themselves upright, especially when blown around in spring rainstorms. Individual wood or metal stakes can help prevent breakage. Bamboo canes painted green and the straight woody suckers pruned off old fruit trees look most natural, blending in well with the foliage. Tie the perennial stem to the stake loosely with twine, leaving some slack for stem movement in the wind. Green or tan twine is less conspicuous than white string.

Some manufactured metal stakes come equipped with a loop at the top, designed to grab and hold a lily stem.

161 Use linking stakes, hoops, and cages to buttress floppy perennials. Linking stakes shaped like upside-down Ls are designed for you to assemble. Join as many segments as you need to surround each floppy perennial that needs support. Standard tomato cages and cylinders constructed of chicken wire or wire fencing can also serve the same purpose. If you have the time, make your own wooden cages by sticking stakes all around the perennial clump and looping twine from stake to stake to circle the frame.

Metal hoop supports are very useful for supporting peonies. They look like oversized steering wheels on legs. Stick the legs in the ground and let the peony grow up through the hoop. I like gridded hoops, which offer extra support to individual peony stems.

162 **The best time to stake perennials is when they first emerge from the ground.** Early in the season you can clearly see the size of perennial clumps and observe where each shoot originates. It's easiest at that time to poke stakes in the ground at the outside margins without damaging roots and stems. As the plants expand, their leaves will quickly cover the unattractive underpinning.

However, it's never too late to stake. I've learned from seasoned gardeners to construct crossed swords–two sturdy straight stakes stuck in the ground at a 45-degree angle, leaning against each other in the shape of an X. They make an emergency mini fence in front of a perennial that's threatening to topple over.

163 **Construct low homemade fences at the front of borders where perennials are about to lean into the lawn.** Borrow some ideas from Japanese gardens to help keep autumn-flowering sedums (*Sedum spectabile*), dwarf asters, and the like in their place. These plants start out modestly but burgeon alarmingly as the season progresses. Small fences made of apple suckers stuck in the ground and shaped into overlapping arches or squat bamboo stakes lashed together with black twine to make a low barrier can be useful and decorative.

You could also place ready-made foot-high cedar picket fences sold in two-foot lengths toward the front of a border where extra support is needed.

You could also place ready-made foot-high cedar picket fences sold in two-foot lengths toward the front of a border where extra support is needed.

Weeding

164 **Weed early in the season to prevent a jungle later on.** Not only will weeding make you feel virtuous, but it's just plain practical to eliminate weeds before they flower, go to seed, and multiply. Pulling out one cress plant will save you the trouble of weeding out hundreds of future seedlings. Trowel out creeping buttercup and you've spared your garden of galloping dozens.

It's not that there's anything wrong with weeds—it's just that it's a competitive world out there, with limited space, and your polite perennials will be elbowed out by more rambunctious plants. It's a matter of choice. Which do you prefer to grow–bellflowers or buttercups? Dandelions or delphiniums?

165 Mulch and plant tightly to minimize weeds. A topdressing of compost or even grass clippings in the bare spaces between perennials will help smother annual seedlings lurking at ground level. Mulch will also keep the ground moist, so that any seeds that blow in and germinate will be that much easier to pull out.

Planting perennials close to each other helps reduce the amount of open ground–any bare dirt is a welcome mat for weeds. This means that you'll probably need to divide your perennials sooner than if you'd spaced them further apart. Another way to cover the ground while your perennials are filling out is to plant self-sowing annuals such as cosmos and love-in-a-mist.

Grooming

166 Cut back leggy fall-blooming perennials early in the season to make them stockier. Many of the tall perennials that bloom late in the season tend to grow lanky and flop over.

Michaelmas daisies (*Aster novi-belgii*), chrysanthemums, boltonia (*Boltonia asteroides*), and sneezeweeds (*Helenium autumnale*) are especially prone to this problem. To solve the difficulty, give them a good shearing in June, cutting them back to about a foot from the ground. This will cause each stem to branch out, thickening the plant so that it will stand on its own feet at bloom time.

167 Cut back stringy spring-blooming perennials after they bloom to thicken the foliage. Many early bloomers, such as snow-in-summer (*Cerastium tomentosum*), cottage pinks (*Dianthus plumarius*), and evergreen candytuft (*Iberis sempervirens*) become spindly after they bloom. You can deadhead and rejuvenate these perennials in one fell swoop. Grab a handful of lanky stems and give them a good haircut, cutting to about six inches from the ground. Existing stems will branch out and new stems will sprout at ground level, renewing the foliage and refreshing the overall appearance of these perennials for summer and fall.

168 Some spent perennials may be cut clear back to the ground to renew their foliage. When oriental poppies (*Papaver orientale*), lady's mantles

(*Alchemilla mollis*), daylilies (*Hemerocallis* species and hybrids), speedwells (*Veronica* species and hybrids), cranesbills (*Geranium* species and hybrids), spiderworts (*Tradescantia virginiana*), globe thistles (*Echinops ritro*), and Siberian iris (*Iris sibirica*) start looking spent and shabby in midsummer, cut their foliage back to the ground. Within a few weeks, fresh new leaves will immensely improve the plant's appearance.

In the case of lady's mantle, globe thistle, spiderwort, and *Veronica longifolia*, new flower buds will also form and you will be rewarded by a second surge of color.

169 Deadhead perennials to improve their appearance and maximize the bloom period. When it comes to once-blooming perennials, removing spent flowers is cosmetic only, for the benefit of the plant's overall appearance. Shabby old flowers detract from the beauty of fresh blooms. This is especially important when plants are placed for close-up viewing, for example, near an entry or patio.

Reblooming perennials such as purple coneflower (*Echinacea purpurea*) and speedwell (*Veronica longifolia*) don't rebloom as well if they're not deadheaded. Once they go to seed, from the plant's point of view, the season is over. Keep them groomed to keep them blooming, taking care not to cut off the newly developing flower stalks. Look carefully at the stems and cut off the old flowers just above the new side buds that produce the next bloom surge.

170 Dig a six-inch ditch between your beds and borders and the lawn to keep the grass from creeping into the flower beds. Use a sharpened half-moon edger or square-edged spade to dig a crisp six-inch trench separating your perennial beds from turf. This will make future edging and mowing easier and keep the outline of your bed nicely defined.

Some gardeners construct a mowing curb made of bricks, pavers, flat stones, or poured concrete. One wheel of the mower can ride along this curb, making lawn maintenance easier.

171 Grow ground covers under the canopy of trees or between vigorous established shrubs, but keep them out of perennial borders. Beginning gardeners especially are likely to mistake ground covers for perennials. Although many ground covers are perennial, returning year after year, they travel rapidly and cover more ground than is practical within the limits of flower beds. Because these ground covers are so prolific, experienced gardeners with an overflow often pass them along to new gardeners, who are eager for free plants. These gifts should come with warning tags that say "Spreads rapidly; plant only in wild areas!"

Here's a list of rampant growers that can be troublesome to their neighbors: bugleweed (*Ajuga reptans*), periwinkle (*Vinca minor*), lily-of-the-valley (*Convallaria majalis*), sweet woodruff (*Asperula odorata*), Labrador viola (*Viola labradorica*), *Geranium* 'Claridge Druce', *Geranium endressii*, bouncing Bet (*Saponaria officinalis*), cypress spurge (*Euphorbia cyparissias*), Mrs. Robb's spurge (*Euphorbia robbiae*), spring cinquefoil (*Potentilla verna*), *Potentilla recta*, *Campanula alliariifolia*, *Campanula portenschlagiana*, *Campanula poscharskyana*, self-heal (*Prunella vulgaris*), tansy (*Tanacetum vulgare*), creeping St. Johnswort (*Hypericum calycinum*).

172 Fill the gaps between new plants with moderately spreading perennials that are easy to remove later on.** Lady's mantle (*Alchemilla mollis*), bloody cranesbill (*Geranium sanguineum*), and feverfew (*Chrysanthemum parthenium*) have been faithful fillers that suppress weeds while my daylilies, peonies, and Siberian iris filled out. Gradually I've dug out the extra fillers and moved them to new beds where they served the same ground-covering purpose.

173 **Carefully cut back the spent foliage of evergreen perennials just before the new leaves emerge.** If you wait to cut back the old foliage of western sword fern or autumn fern until after the new croziers have unfurled, inevitably you'll snip off some new fronds by accident. Groom the plant early in spring before the new growth emerges to prevent such disaster.

Cut back last year's bishop's hat's (*Epimedium*) leaves in winter before the early spring foliage and flower stems emerge. That way you won't have to strain your eyes to distinguish between old foliage, new leaves, and newly emerging flower stems. Groom last year's tattered Lenten rose (*Helleborus orientalis)* foliage in early winter, just as the new flower buds at ground level show color, before they rise on their stems and get tangled up with the old leaves.

174 **While waiting to place a perennial, pot it up in an ample container, or plant it in a holding bed.**

Often I buy before I plan, and while I figure out where to plant my new treasure, I pot it up into a larger container with rich soil. That way it can spread its roots out almost as well as it would in the ground, instead of being cramped in its original nursery pot.

A friend plants her new perennials in the vegetable garden until she's ready to commit to a spot in the border. That way the perennial can take advantage of the fertile, well-prepared soil and develop while waiting for a more permanent home.

175 When in doubt about a definite place to plant a perennial, sink it in the ground, pot and all, and watch it for a while. I learned this labor-saving tip from garden writer Pamela Harper. Instead of planting a perennial and changing your mind, only to dig it up and disturb the root system, try it on for size right in the container. Prepare your planting hole as usual, and settle your potted perennial in place.

Make sure that the pot has plenty of drainage holes before sinking it into the planting space. Study it as part of the composition for as long as you like until you're sure it fits in. If it does, unpot it and plant it permanently. If it doesn't, pull it out and try another plant.

Coping with Pests and Weather

176 Trap slugs by setting out boards or upside-down grapefruit shells. Slugs naturally gather under any cool, dark, damp shelter—you'll find them under rocks or beneath big leaves. If you make a perfect shelter for them by putting out a few boards or the husks of grapefruits, you'll know exactly where to find them and dispose of them in the morning.

177 Keep a container handy to separate slugs from your prize hostas and ligularias. Over the years I've bought my share of slug bait—until a veterinary bill (my cat tasted the bait) and a hard look at the cumulative expense of pesticide made me change my methods.

Now I slip on surgical gloves and collect slugs when they're most visible—early in the morning and late in the evening—and plunk them into an old coffee can, then slam the lid on. Some gardeners use a plastic milk jug with the top cut off and a little ammonia and water in the bottom. Long-handled tongs are helpful for collecting.

178 **The thicker the hosta leaf, the better it will resist slugs.** It's so embarrassing to have hostas full of holes. To lessen the likelihood of slugs dining on the tender leaves, choose hostas with heavy substance or thick leaves.

For blue-leaved selections, try 'Abiqua Trumpet', 'Big Daddy', 'Big Mama', 'Crinoline Petticoats', 'Hadspen Blue', 'Krossa Regal', and 'Royal Quilt'. Gold-leaved hostas with thick leaves include 'Zounds', 'Vanilla Cream', 'Sum and Substance', 'Treasure', 'Shade Master', and 'Bright Glow'. Impressive 'Christmas Tree' has large, wide, deep green leaves with creamy white edges. For a complete chart of hostas listing their height, color, texture, substance, leaf shape, flower color, and form, write to Robyn's Nest Nursery, 7802 NE 63rd Street, Vancouver, WA 98662, for a Hosta Cross Reference Chart ($5).

179 **Protect your half-hardy perennials from dessicating winter wind with prunings from needle evergreens.** Recycle your Christmas tree: cut up the boughs and lay them loosely over the top of perennials that are marginally hardy to your zone to give them that extra edge of protection. For perennials that are tall or brittle, stick some boughs in the ground vertically all around the clump to make a little frame, and rest a few over the top to gently enclose the perennial.

180 **Be flexible: respect the limitations of the weather for the best results.** In early spring when it's been pouring down rain and the soil is sodden, don't try to turn the soil–you'll just make a muddy mess. Instead, don your raingear and do some pruning, or organize your toolshed.

In the heat of summer, garden early in the morning or late in the evening when it's cool. If you must work while it's blazing hot, give yourself a break and keep cool in the shadier borders.

181 **Perennial borders will have their peak moments. Enjoy them and accept the in-between lulls and lapses.** Times of perfection in the garden are rare and wonderful. On a few choice days all comes together in a harmony of colors–roses, delphiniums, foxgloves, and bellflowers opening triumphantly at the same time. Savor those culminations. And understand that one hard rainstorm can splatter the peonies with mud and shatter the newly opened roses. Sudden gaps will appear in a border where a plant died or a pet took a nap. Don't freak out. Enjoy the process of tending and shaping the whole picture, complete with its ups and downs.

Save Yourself!

182 Pack a small carryall with essential gardening supplies to save trips back and forth to the toolshed. I like the small plastic baskets that you find in grocery stores with convenient, fold-down handles. A canvas tote or a wicker basket with a sturdy handle for carrying will work too. Move it around the garden as you work, with the following items stored inside: four small containers, one with bonemeal, one with liquid fertilizer, one with granular slow-release fertilizer, and one with lime; a zippered plastic storage bag full of plant labels, marking pencils, and a writing pad for reminder notes to yourself; a small folding saw, hand pruners, and a narrow trowel; a selection of gloves (leather, cotton, surgical); a roll of twine for tying vines; sunscreen and insect repellent.

183 Recycle household items for handy storage of garden supplies. Save plastic honey dispensers and shampoo bottles for storing manageable amounts of liquid fertilizer–that way you won't have to lug gallon jugs around the garden. Use lidded yogurt containers to hold dry supplies–bonemeal, blood meal, lime. . . . Plastic berry baskets are perfect for keeping seed packets upright and storing small bulbs. Old film canisters are great for saving dry seed.

184 Hang a pair of hand pruners and a small trowel on your belt. I never set foot in the garden without two indispensable tools—a pair of Felco #2 hand pruners for deadheading and pruning and a narrow trowel for weeding. (Without the trowel I yank out weeds without getting their roots, a futile task.) It's easy to find a leather holster for hand pruners with slits at the top for threading a belt through. To find one the right size for a narrow trowel, look in the tool section of a hardware store (mine was intended to be an awl holder).

To save time, thread an old belt with your hand pruners and trowel and keep it in the toolshed. That way it's ready for you to strap on at a moment's notice.

185 Instead of buying expensive gardener's gear, buy comfortable clothing in the pharmacy and at fishing supply stores. The best gloves I've ever used are disposable surgical gloves. Waterproof yet thin enough for good finger dexterity, surgical gloves come in handy boxes of 100. Yes, they tear after a few hours of hard use, but they're inexpensive.

An old fishing vest purchased at a sporting goods store has many small pockets perfect for labels, twine, marking pencils, and seed packets. Fishermen's boots and slickers and workmen's cotton shirts and pants are also much less costly than those made exclusively for gardeners.

186 Although heavy-duty hoses last forever, if they're hard on your back, buy lighter ones. Most of us want hoses to last forever, but let's face it, if they're too heavy to haul around, our bodies will suffer. It's more economical to replace your hoses every few years than injure your back from continuously dragging heavy hoses around the garden.

187 Keep the weight at the front of your wheelbarrow for easiest navigation. Put sacks of fertilizer or heavy plants at the nose end of your barrow where the weight will help propel it forward. When loading compost, fork more dirt toward the front end.

When moving gravel or damp sand, give yourself a break by filling the barrow only half full and make more frequent, manageable trips.

188 Wear waterproof rubber or latex gloves when tending spurges (*Euphorbia* species and hybrids) and rue (*Ruta graveolens*) to protect your skin. When cut, spurges and rue exude a milky sap that can be irritating to your skin and eyes. Be careful to wear gloves when gardening around these plants, and don't touch your eyes. The juice from these plants can make your eyes tear for hours.

189 Avoid pesticides and herbicides if you want to attract birds and butterflies to your garden. Pesticides poison insects, destroying a major food source for the birds. Some butterflies lay their eggs in the lawn, and a dose of weed killer will destroy the next generation. The same chemical that kills cutworms will also harm butterfly larva. Instead of indiscriminately killing insects, use mechanical means to deter the bad guys. To keep cutworms from decapitating young plants, surround the crown with a cardboard collar or hand-pick the villains at night.

Propagation

Seeds

190 **For the greatest economy, start perennials from seed in sterile potting soil.** One package of perennial seed costs less than a small plant and will give you dozens of starts, provided the seed is fresh. However, you may have to wait two years from germination to bloom time. Use as much seed as you need and store the packet in the refrigerator to keep the leftovers viable.

Blend your own soil mix from equal parts of perlite, vermiculite, and peat moss or save time by buying bagged, sterile potting soil. Look for loose, crumbly soil and avoid mixtures that resemble bark dust. Fill four-inch pots or seedling trays from last year's annuals with soil, set these in a tray, and water the pots from below. A small amount of fungicide in the water (I use a one-fourth strength solution) will help prevent damping off, a fungal disease the kills seedlings. Note the name and date on a plastic label inserted in your pot at planting time—you'd be surprised how hard it is to identify perennials seedlings before they bloom.

191 Give seedlings warmth, darkness, and consistent moisture to get them off to a good start. I start my seedlings in opaque plastic sweater boxes, shutting the lids firmly so that the interior stays dark and damp. I found an ideal place for these boxes—between the top of a freezer and a heating duct in the basement, where it's nice and warm. I've also stored them under the sofa, near a floor heating vent.

If you don't want to invest in plastic boxes, create a minigreenhouse by enclosing a tray or flat in a big plastic bag. Stick a couple of pencils or chopsticks into the tray to create headroom so that the newly sprouting seedlings won't get mashed. As soon as the seedlings germinate, take the lid off the box or slip the plastic bag off the tray.

192 Place your newly sprouted seedlings in the best light possible for compact growth. A greenhouse is ideal for the maximum light, and a sunny windowsill is good too. But you can also grow plants indoors under fluorescent lights. I use shop lights suspended from chains that are attached to hooks in the ceiling. S-hooks between the fixture and the chains allow me to adjust the chains as the seedlings grow taller. I keep the seedlings six inches away from the lights so that they grow steadily and compactly. A plant much further away from a source of light will grow leggy.

For years I kept the lights on for 16 hours a day, but when my timers broke I left the lights on constantly and the plants thrived. At first I was careful to use one cool and one warm fluorescent light in each fixture, following instructions from a magazine, but when I used standard fluorescent bulbs the plants flourished too. The key is to experiment and learn, instead of following ironclad rules.

193 Start your seedlings about two months before your planting date. Most seedlings need anywhere from two days to two weeks to germinate. (There are exceptions that need special treatment, and a good reference book will inform you about the tricks of the trade.) Six more weeks are enough time for a young plant to develop before leaping into the garden. During this early growth period indoors, feed your seedlings weekly with a quarter-strength dilution of 20-20-20 fertilizer—you'll practically see the leaves grow. Water from below in order not to damage the fragile young plants.

Divisions

194 **The best time to divide established perennials is early spring or late fall.** When perennials first leaf out you can lift and divide them without doing damage to developing stems or buds. The same is true in late fall when the plants are past their flowering period. When dividing in fall, cut back spent foliage first to make the job more manageable.

Dividing in spring is less risky, as your new starts will have spring, summer, and fall to develop strong roots and settle in before winter hits. I've sometimes lost divisions planted in fall when winter storms blast the young plants before they've had a chance to settle in.

195 **Two wheelbarrows are handy at dividing time—one full of compost to backfill the holes, and one for tools, a bucket of bonemeal, and a tarp.** When you're digging up plants it's easy to forget the locations of the holes you've left behind. Take a wheelbarrow of well-rotted compost with you and backfill the gaps as you go. Shovel your compost from the back of the wheelbarrow, and heel your new divisions into this same compost at the front of the wheelbarrow, to prevent their roots from drying out.

Store a border fork, a large shovel, and a pickax in a second wheelbarrow so that you'll have all the necessary tools on hand when you need them. Add a bucket of bonemeal to use when planting the new divisions and a tarp upon which to divide your perennials.

196 Loosen the soil around established perennials with a border fork, then lift the clump out of the ground and onto a tarp to divide it into sections. You can probe the ground more gently with a fork than with a spade–it's easy to sever stems from their roots with a spade that accidentally slips. Pry all around the edges of a clump and loosen the earth, then gradually ease the plant out of the ground. You may need to make several sweeps around the edges of a big perennial, and rock the plant a bit before it comes loose.

Lift the clump onto a tarp laid out on the lawn or sidewalk–that way you can move freely without crashing into nearby plants. The tarp will also make this job tidier by catching loose soil, old leaves, and any spent or woody parts of the perennial. You can pull apart perennials with shallow root systems without much effort, taking care that each division has stems attached to roots.

197 Carry an empty flat, a few labels, and a waterproof marking pencil when taking divisions. Put your new divisions in the flat, and add a label noting the plant's name and date. You'd be surprised how easily small perennial segments get confused with debris in the middle of a tarp. It's also easy to mistake a plant's identity when the only clue is a little foliage and some roots. Dating the labels will also help you learn how soon these divisions grow into mature plants.

198 To divide large clumps of densely rooted perennials, first cut the foliage back to about a foot, then get your ax out. When it comes to established plants with dense root systems, such as Siberian or Spuria iris, daylilies, and ornamental grasses, get ready for some work. These are tough customers that call for strong tools and some muscle. A mattock with a double-sided blade is ideal–one side is a pick; the other is an ax. Loosen the soil around the perennial clump with the pick, then dig it out with a large shovel. Lay it on its side on a tarp and whack it into four or more sections with the ax blade.

Don't worry about being exact—you're bound to cut through stems and roots, butchering some of the plant as you chop, but you'll still have plenty of viable divisions. I begin by dividing the clump in half, then into quarters, and if those are still too hefty to move, into eighths. Each piece can be replanted or potted up. Be sure to water the newly planted divisions well.

199 To take divisions without disturbing the entire plant, dig small sections from around the edges of a large clump. It's totally harmless to sneak small segments away from a mother plant, just as long as you're able to dig out well-rooted stems. Cranesbills, gooseneck loosestrife, and many other perennials that spread by creeping can be divided this way.

Lift the edges of the perennials away from the clump with a fork and pull away enough material for a new plant. Cut the roots or rhizomes away from the mother plant with sharp, hand-held pruning shears. Backfill the hole with well-rotted compost and your original plant will quickly spread out to fill the gap.

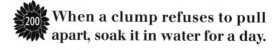 **200 When a clump refuses to pull apart, soak it in water for a day.**

Sometimes daylilies or hostas are so densely rooted that it's hard to find a place to pry them apart. Grab a bucket or tub (without drainage holes) big enough to house the plant, plunk it in, and add enough water to cover the root zone. This will wash away and loosen the soil, allowing you to separate the divisions more easily the next day.

Suggested Reading

Armitage, Allan M. *Herbaceous Perennial Plants.* Athens, GA: Varsity Press, Inc., 1989.

Bath, Trevor and Joy Jones. *The Gardener's Guide to Growing Hardy Geraniums.* Portland, OR: Timber Press, 1994.

Bloom, Alan. *Perennials for Your Garden.* Chicago: Floraprint U.S., 1981.

Chatto, Beth. *The Green Tapestry.* London: HarperCollins Publishers, 1989.

Clausen, Ruth Rogers and Nicolas H. Eckstrom. *Perennials for American Gardens.* New York: Random House, 1989.

Harper, Pamela J. *Color Echoes.* New York: Macmillan Publishing Company, 1994.

Harper, Pamela J. *Designing with Perennials*. New York: Macmillan Publishing Company, 1994.

Hobhouse, Penelope. *Color in Your Garden*. Boston: Little, Brown and Company, 1985.

Hudak, Joseph. *Gardening with Perennials*. Portland, OR: Timber Press, 1985.

Rix, Martyn and Roger Phillips. *Perennials*. New York: Random House, Inc., 1991.

Taylor, Nigel J. *Ornamental Grasses, Bamboos, Rushes and Sedges*. London: Ward Lock Limited, 1992.

Thomas, Graham Stuart. *Perennial Garden Plants*. London: J. M. Dent & Sons Ltd., 1976.

Wilson, Helen Van Pelt and Leonie Bell. *The Fragrant Year*. New York: William Morrow & Co., Inc., 1967.

Sources for
Perennials

Although it's nearly impossible to stay current about mail-order sources with nurseries going in and out of business and moving, I'd still like to list at least these few to expand your perennial palette. When sending for a catalog, it's a good idea to include a few dollars to cover the cost of printing and mailing. For a more complete directory, see the current edition of Barbara J. Barton's *Gardening by Mail.*

Ambergate Gardens, 8015 Krey Avenue, Waconia, MN 55387-9616, 612-443-2248.

B & D Lilies, 330 P Street, Port Townsend, WA 98368, 360-385-1738.

Kurt Bluemel (grasses, aquatics), 2740 Green Lane, Baldwin, MD 21013.

Bluestone Perennials, 7211 Middle Ridge Road, Madison, OH 44057, 800-852-5243.

Busse Gardens, 5873 Oliver Avenue SW, Cokato, MN 55321-3601, 800-544-3192.

Canyon Creek Nursery, 3527 Dry Creek Road, Oroville, CA 95965, 916-533-2166.

Caprice Farm Nursery (peonies, daylilies, Japanese iris), 15425 SW Pleasant Hill Road, Sherwood, OR 97140, 503-625-7241.

Collector's Nursery, 16804 NE 102 Avenue, Battle Ground, WA 98604, 360-574-3832.

Dutch Gardens (bulbs), POB 200, Adelphia, NJ 07710-0200, 201-780-2713.

Englerth Gardens (daylilies, hostas, iris), 2461 22 Street, Hopkins, MI 49328, 616-793-7196.

Fancy Fronds (ferns), 1911 4th Avenue West, Seattle, WA 98119-2610, 206-284-5332.

ForestFarm Nursery (trees, shrubs, perennials), 990 Tetherow Road, Williams, OR 97544-9599, 541-846-7269.

Gardens of the Blue Ridge, Box 10, Pineola, NC 28662, 704-733-2417.

Heronswood Nursery,
7530 288th Street NE, Kingston,
WA 98346, 360-297-4172.

Joy Creek Nursery,
20300 NW Watson Road, Scapoose,
OR 97056, 503-227-2160.

Klehm Nursery (daylilies, peonies,
hostas), 4210 N. Duncan Road,
Champaign, IL 61821, 800-553-3715.

Laurie's Gardens (Japanese,
Siberian iris), 41886 McKenzie
Highway, Springfield, OR 97377,
503-896-3756.

Niche Gardens, Route 1, Box 290,
Chapel Hill, NC 27516, 919-967-0078.

Piccadilly Farm (hostas, hellebores),
1971 Whippoorwill Road, Bishop,
GA 30621, 404-769-6516.

Robyn's Nest (hostas),
7802 NE 63rd Street, Vancouver,
WA 98662, 360-256-7399.

Rocknoll Nursery, 9210 U.S. 50,
Hillsboro, OH 45133, 513-393-1278.

Siskiyou Rare Plant Nursery,
2825 Cummings Road, Medford,
OR 97501, 541-772-6846.

Wayside Gardens, Hodges, SC
29695-0001, 800-845-1124.

We-Du Nursery, Route 5, Box 724, Marion, NC 28752, 704-738-8300.

White Flower Farm, Litchfield, CT 06759-0050, 203-567-0801.

The Wildwood Flower (*Lobelia cardinalis* hybrids), Route 3, Box 165, Pittsboro, NC 27312.

Yucca Do Nursery, Box 655, Waller, TX 77484.

Index

I

J

Rudbeckia
> 'Goldquelle', yellow coneflower, 121
>
> 'Goldsturm', black–eyed Susan, 121, 132
>
> *R. nitida*, coneflower, 121, 141
>
> *R. triloba*, brown–eyed Susan, 83, 132

rue, *Ruta graveolens*, 55, 69, 188

Russian sage, *Perovskia atriplicifolia*, 52, 119, 137, 140, 155

Ruta graveolens, rue, 55, 69, 188

S

sage, 56. *See also Salvia.*

St. Johnswort, *Hypericum calycinum*, 171

Salvia, sage
> 'Victoria Blue' 90
>
> *S. patens*, 76, 119
>
> *S. pitcherii*, 76
>
> *S. uliginosa*, 76

Santa Barbara daisy, *Erigeron karvinskianus*, 50, 107, 154

santolina, 89

Saponaria officinalis, bouncing Bet, 171

sawdust, 18

Saxifraga umbrosa, London pride, 57, 68

Scabiosa, pincushion flower
> *S. caucasica*, 140
>
> *S. ochroleuca*, 37, 132, 133

Schizostylis coccinea, kaffir lily, 132, 140

Sedum, 65, 124, 157
> 'Mohrchen' 56, 109
>
> 'Rosy Glow' 157
>
> 'Ruby Glow' 127, 157
>
> 'Vera Jameson' 123, 157
>
> *S. alboroseum* 'Medio-Variegatum' 62
>
> *S. sieboldii*, 108, 123, 157

T

and mulches, 18, 19, 20
weevils, 25
wheelbarrows, 187, 195
whiteflies, 22, 25
willow gentian, *Gentiana asclepiadea,*
    76, 91
winter bloomers, 67, 110, 114–16
winter cyclamen, *Cyclamen coum,* 115, 128
wood mulches and nitrogen, 18
woodland gardens, 60, 61, 72, 115
wooly thyme, *Sedum spathulifolium,* 59

Y

yarrow, 48, 73, 74. *See also Achillea.*

Z

Zauschneria californica, fuschia, 142
zebra grass, *Miscanthus sinensis*
    'Zebrinus', 123, 150
zinnia, 53